CORPORATION
· FOR ·
ENTERPRISE
DEVELOPMENT

THE 1994 DEVELOPMENT REPORT CARD FOR THE STATES

ECONOMIC

BENCHMARKS

FOR STATE

AND

CORPORATE

DECISION-

MAKERS

Eighth

Edition

ISSN: 1045-4691
ISBN: 1-883187-01-X
Library of Congress Catalog Number: 93-70699

CORPORATION
· FOR ·
ENTERPRISE
DEVELOPMENT

National Office
777 North Capitol Street, NE
Suite 80l
Washington, DC 20002
Phone: (202) 408-9788
Fax: (202) 408-9793

Foreword

This is the eighth edition of *The Development Report Card for the States* and an important one for CFED. This year, we return to the Report Card origins and the stance we took back in 1986 questioning commonly held assumptions about what it takes to improve a state's business climate. Both policymakers and practitioners have suggested to us on a number of occasions that CFED can "declare victory" insofar as the Report Card has changed the terms of the debate about what is important in economic development. Many have said that most states no longer rely solely on attraction strategies but increasingly focus on encouraging indigenous development; that the pursuit of high wage, high skills jobs is now axiomatic; that states look less towards finding quick-fix solutions and now concern themselves with longer-term investments in human capital and physical, financial, and technological infrastructure. They have encouraged us to believe that the Report Card is *the* benchmarking tool against which most state policymakers and legislators measure their performance year by year.

Unfortunately, much as we would love to accept all this as the truth, there is a great deal of evidence to show that we still have a long way to go. Business climate has become a hot topic of debate in every state. In spite of the fact that they are facing substantial structural budget deficits, states are being asked to reduce taxes, requiring dramatic cutbacks on public services. This is increasingly being justified on the basis of improving business climate through reducing business costs, even though services upon which business relies – education, transportation, waste disposal – are being undermined.

Yet at the same time, in response to pressure to do "something" about the economy as companies continue to downsize and unemployment remains stubbornly high, states find themselves joining the race to attract companies to locate in their area. The race has become so competitive that states have been willing to give away millions of dollars in tax incentives and development costs, with the latest round of automobile assembly plants pushing the cost per job beyond $200,000. In our new publication, *Bidding for Business: Are Cities and States Selling Themselves Short?*, we explore this issue in some detail and offer some ways out of the wasteful bidding wars.

Both trends are damaging to the long-term health of states and the country as a whole. They sacrifice long-term development for short-term gain; they reduce the ability of a state to deliver effective and quality public services; and they herald a return to the proposition that low wages, low taxes, and lax environmental regulations are the main determinants of a good business climate.

We continue to publish the Report Card and use it as a means of stimulating debate about these issues. Each year we try to improve its accessibility in terms of presentation and content. What remains constant however, is that the framework of measures and the sources we use are fully disclosed so that anyone can replicate the calculations or add weights to different indices to test their robustness. We use the same measures each year, as far as data availability allows, so that assessments can be made about a state's performance over time.

CFED differs from many research institutes and think tanks as it is based on the belief that it is important to test policy ideas in the field through consulting, technical assistance, and training activities. These applied efforts constitute CFED's "laboratories" where we test new approaches, evaluate their viability, generate new ideas, and discard those that are not viable. We also believe that a state's economy should be measured in terms both of competitiveness and of equity; a polarized economy does not offer a healthy business climate.

The Report Card is our effort to provide a good source of comparative data for the field, based upon what we have learned in our work, and a way to encourage states to review their economic development policies against a broader set of criteria than might otherwise be the case.

The Report Card has never been unduly influenced by corporate foundation or union funding; by any particular state and/or its development and political officials; by its subscribers; or by the media. The views expressed here are entirely our own. That said, we would like to gratefully acknowledge the support of those forward-looking corporations, foundations, and unions who have subscribed to a broader view of economic development these past eight years. We also gratefully acknowledge the support of the hundreds of purchasers of *The Development Report Card for the States*.

Brian Dabson
President
Corporation for Enterprise Development
Washington, DC, 1994

Table of Contents

State Report Cards (continued)

Introduction

The 1994 Development Report Card for the States

The Development Report Card for the States is an annual assessment of the strengths and weaknesses of each state's economy and its potential for future growth using state-by-state comparisons based upon over 50 socioeconomic data measures. The Report Card's methodology is a comparative one in which each state's performance is evaluated in terms of the performance of all the others. This type of assessment, called *comparative benchmarking*, is very powerful in its ability to take into account broad macroeconomic cycles and to highlight strengths and weaknesses. For example, is a state's moderate employment growth over the last couple of years actually a positive sign if all others are growing at twice the rate? Doesn't that imply that this state is lagging behind?

The Report Card compares and grades all states in each of three indexes measuring different aspects of its economic health, supplemented by a general rating of its tax and fiscal system's ability to support long-term economic development. The indexes are structured to measure:

Economic Performance: *How many economic benefits and opportunities is the state economy providing its populace?*

Business Vitality: *How vital and dynamic is the state's business sector?*

Development Capacity: *What is the state's capacity for future growth and recovery from economic adversity?*

Each of these graded indexes is comprised of three or more subindexes, also graded, providing a more detailed understanding of the facets of a state's economy. The exception is the Environmental, Social & Health Conditions Subindex which is not graded.

Because the Tax & Fiscal Index compares financial systems, not economic outcomes, and because relevant data is often not as precise and as frequently updated, we do not grade the Tax & Fiscal Index as we do the three main economic indexes. Rather, the states are ranked and given a plus for an exemplary system, a minus for a poor one, and a check for those in the middle.

The Report Card's framework is based upon two key assumptions. The first is that the goal of any state development policy is increased economic well-being for its citizens. The second is that businesses flourish in healthy economies and not in poor, stagnant ones. Thus the goals of state development officials and the business community are complementary. Policymakers want a strong economy to fulfill their public mandate. Businesses want to be in a healthy economy as a means of encouraging their own economic success.

The success of a state's economy depends upon the vitality of its businesses and the strength of its physical infrastructure and human, financial, and technological resources. There is not a direct, simple causal relationship between development capacity, business vitality, and economic performance because there are too many external forces beyond the control of state or federal government affecting national and regional economies and the activities of individual businesses. Nevertheless, there is a strong correlation between them, especially between economic performance and development capacity. States with the requisite resources can better develop competitive, dynamic, and vital businesses – the underpinning of future economic prosperity.

The Report Card's three indexes reflect this relationship.

It is important to realize that a state's position in each of the three indexes changes at different paces. Economic Performance can exhibit noticeable annual changes, and Business Vitality can swing dramatically in a single year. Yet Development Capacity, the fundamentals, takes much longer to grow and flourish. Ironically, it is this slowest moving index which is most susceptible to direct policy intervention. Business Vitality can be affected but much less directly than resource development, and Economic Performance is almost impossible to directly impact via specific policies. Yet it is the investments in development capacity, made for the long haul, which can lead to stronger, more sustainable performance and recovery.

The Tax & Fiscal System Index measures how well-equipped a state's financial system is to provide solid support for future economic development. A balanced, equitable, and stable tax and fiscal system is required to sustain long-term investments and help minimize uncertainties. As the National Conference of State Legislatures and the National Governors' Association write:

> "...generally acknowledged principles of good state tax policy...hold that a state tax system should provide appropriate and timely revenues, distribute burdens equitably, promote economic efficiency and growth, be easily administered and ensure accountability." (*Financing State Government in the 1990's*, 1993, page vii)

In contrast, escalating tax incentives and giveaways have had a mixed record, at best, in creating jobs and landing companies – usually successful only when all other factors and resources are equal and also often at great financial cost (see *Bidding for Business*, CFED, 1994; *Financing State Government in the 1990's*, chapter 5; and the Tax & Fiscal System Index).

Results, Not Just Efforts

Unlike many other studies, such as the old Grant Thornton Manufacturing Index and the Cato Institute's recent judgment on states' fiscal strategies, the Report Card is built on outcome-based measures. It shows how healthy a state's economy actually is, not how hard everyone has worked at improving it. Thus, the Report Card measures an increase in employment, *not* the number of business recruitment offices in a state; it measures the increase in new businesses and *not* new tax incentives being offered; and it measures the education of the workforce, *not* the availability and quality of training. Knowing what and how well states are practicing economic development is important, but it is not the bottom line. Instead, the Report Card concentrates on the differences these efforts make to both citizens and business.

As a result, the Report Card does not distinguish between states that are conscientiously investing in the future and those that are coasting off their past. Many states that currently rank at the bottom of the Development Capacity Index are actually among the most active pioneers in education reform, public-private partnerships, and industrial modernization. Their efforts are making them exciting places to live, work, and grow a business, but the results of their initiatives may not show up in the aggregate statistics for perhaps even another decade.

As airwaves and business journals once again are filled with oratory that taxes and government spending, ipso facto, extinguish business growth, it is important to remain focused on outcome-based measures. The difference in these two approaches is illustrated in the very different assessments of Minnesota by the Report Card and the Cato Institute's *Fiscal Policy Report Card on America's Governors* (1994). The Cato Institute report, consisting simply of five expenditure variables (gross state spending per family and changes over time) and nine tax and revenue measures (changes in the gross tax burden and revenue collections as well as changes in four specific kinds of taxes), simply declares that, "virtually all of the states with poor economic performance in recent years have governors who have pursued policies of high taxes and spending" (page 2). Yet, many of the best performing states in terms of employment, income growth, and new investment – what most politicians and citizens would consider evidence of good economic performance – were poorly rated in this index. Minnesota is a so-called "tax and spend" state, but it has the sixth strongest Economic Performance rank in the country, and its overall 1994 Report Card grades of two As and a B are surpassed only by Colorado. According to one of Minnesota's leading economists, U.S. manufacturing employment has fallen five percent, but Minnesota's has risen forty percent (telephone interview with Tom Stinson, University of Minnesota, March 1994). The state managed to avoid over-dependence on autos, defense, and textiles and apparel, but they still didn't just "luck out." Their workforce is enormously productive due to strategic, effective investments in education and infrastructure (number one in the country for high school completion, third fewest highway deficiencies, and fifth fewest bridge deficiencies), adding to the state's strength.

The Report Card Framework

The Report Card framework was first developed several years ago based upon an extensive literature review and on the review of a technical advisory board comprised of economic development experts and business, labor, government, and community development officials. Each year we have revised and honed the measures used and the presentation of the book based upon reader response and CFED's own hands-on experience in policy development across the nation.

The core of the Report Card is in the grades and ranks for every state in all three indexes and each individual measure. These are presented on individual state Report Cards at the book's center and summarized in the National Findings. As before, the book presents national and regional findings – the overall patterns and lessons discernible each year for the entire nation and each geographic region – plus detailed source notes and measure descriptions for each index, and an in-depth discussion of the appropriate state tax and fiscal systems for economic development.

Although grades and ranks are given for each subindex and index, no single overall grade is given because it telescopes the complex facets of each state's economy far too much. We give grades because they give a quick and immediate sense of a state's overall comparative position in each area, which can easily be used as a guide to further exploration – both within and outside of the Report Card data – into the complex economic forces at work in each state. They should not be used as an excuse to avoid further investigation.

Who Should Use the Report Card?

The Report Card has been designed as a tool to help people and organizations interested in assessing and evaluating a state's economic progress and development. The Report Card is recommended reading for:

- economic development officials;
- strategic planners;
- elected and appointed officials;
- state and local chambers of commerce:
- utility executives;
- community and labor leaders; and
- corporate site planners.

In short, the Report Card is for everyone who wants to know how a state is doing in providing a healthy economic environment for its citizenry and businesses, or for anyone who wants some initial guidance on what needs to be done for improvement.

How Should the Report Card be Used?

The Report Card does not offer prescriptions, nor does it provide detailed descriptions of individual states and their economic histories. Rather, the Report Card presents a comparative assessment of each state's overall economic performance, the vitality and dynamism in its business community, and the relative strength of its resources necessary for its future economic health, all relative to other states. The Report Card's ranking methodology allows comparison of a state to its neighbors and competitors.

Another way to assess a state's efforts over the years is to compare all of the states in its region using the five-year data in the Regional Findings. This data can also be used to compare a state's economic performance to that of other states with similar development capacity resources and business vitality, illustrating whether a state has fallen behind or overachieved.

Whom do you want to emulate? Find states with similar resource levels in previous years but better economic performance. Why are they doing better? Find the overall leaders in the nation and your geographic region and ask why they are doing so well.

Thinking of expanding your company? How do the states you are considering rate in the resources which are most important to you? How do the states compare in overall economic conditions? How do they compare in relation to their neighbors?

There are a host of other questions to be asked: What have been a particular state's strong points recently? Where is it weakest? Where has it improved or declined dramatically? What do recent changes in Development Capacity and Business Vitality present for the future?

Some warnings: The Report Card is not a crystal ball. It does not predict the future; it only indicates in which direction a state has been traveling and how well it is prepared to meet upcoming challenges. Additionally, the current economic performance indicators do not reflect economic conditions this week, nor last month, but rather over the past year or two. Data collection and time limitations prohibit "real time" evaluation akin to stock prices. Finally, the indicators use data from different years, so care should be taken when comparing individual measures.

The Report Card is best used as a tool to explore important economic questions about where a state's economy is and where it is going.

National Findings

The 1994 Development Report Card

STATE	INDEXES Economic Performance	Business Vitality	Development Capacity	STATE	INDEXES Economic Performance	Business Vitality	Development Capacity
Alabama	C	A	D	Montana	D	B	B
Alaska	A	C	C	Nebraska	A	D	B
Arizona	C	F	B	Nevada	B	C	C
Arkansas	C	D	F	New Hampshire	A	D	C
California	F	C	B	New Jersey	C	A	A
Colorado	A	A	A	New Mexico	D	B	C
Connecticut	B	D	A	New York	D	A	C
Delaware	B	B	B	North Carolina	C	C	D
Florida	C	C	D	North Dakota	D	B	C
Georgia	C	B	C	Ohio	C	C	B
Hawaii	A	F	B	Oklahoma	D	F	D
Idaho	C	A	C	Oregon	B	D	A
Illinois	D	A	A	Pennsylvania	B	B	B
Indiana	A	A	D	Rhode Island	D	F	B
Iowa	A	D	B	South Carolina	D	D	D
Kansas	C	B	C	South Dakota	B	D	D
Kentucky	F	C	F	Tennessee	B	A	D
Louisiana	F	C	F	Texas	C	A	C
Maine	D	B	D	Utah	A	B	A
Maryland	C	C	B	Vermont	B	C	C
Massachusetts	C	C	A	Virginia	B	B	C
Michigan	C	C	C	Washington	B	C	A
Minnesota	A	B	A	West Virginia	F	F	F
Mississippi	D	A	F	Wisconsin	A	D	A
Missouri	F	B	C	Wyoming	C	C	D

For more information on how grades are calculated, see the Methodology section.
For a detailed explanation of indexes, refer to the individual index sections.

The National Story

The Backdrop

The Economy: 1991 and 1992 were sluggish years for the U.S. economy – a sputter after the booming 1980s. By mid-1993 the country had begun its climb out of the recession, but winter saw people still waiting for the traditional post-recession boom. The 1991-1992 recession was unusually long but "mild" with low unemployment, yet after officially ending in spring 1992, the U.S. did not see a rebound in consumer confidence for another three-quarters of a year. This was followed by several more months of "jobless recovery." Meanwhile, according to a report from the Federal Reserve Bank of Dallas, a highly disproportionate share of the economic growth in 1993 was attributable to productivity gains rather than employment. In addition, the early signs suggest that while corporate earnings are on the rise, wages have not followed suit.

These national economic indicators and trends are unsettling, and are putting state officials under great pressure to do something to make their economies grow. Thus, we are seeing an increasing interest in business climate issues. What can states do to get healthy, as the economy does not seem to be improving well enough on its own? How can a state be prepared to weather the next economic storm?

It used to be that business bliss was simply defined as low wages, low taxes, and no "pesky" unions. Impoverished states routinely made the top of business climate indexes such as the Grant Thornton Index (the *Annual Study of General Manufacturing Climates of the Forty-eight Contiguous States of America*) and the more recent Cato Institute fiscal rankings of all state governors. But revolutions in technology and management, and increasing global competition coupled with a growing concern over persistent poverty and income inequality, caused many state leaders to rethink their business development strategies.

It is eight years since CFED developed *The Development Report Card for the States* which broke from the pack. Instead of measuring giveaways, politics, and regulations, the Report Card measures the existing resources necessary for competition in the 21st century – a good workforce, to produce competitively and flexibly; the capital necessary to grow; the technology to stay ahead; the physical infrastructure needed to deliver; the entrepreneurship to innovate; and sectoral diversity and competitive strength to increase market share. Year after year, the Report Card provides ample evidence that the states with the best economic performance are those that invest in their people and physical environment and which have access to adequate fiscal and technical resources.

Government Has a Role: The growing number of anti-tax business climate indexes dovetails with recent calls for government downsizing. But the popular "Reinventing Government" concept calls for efficient and accountable government and the use of public-private partnerships and nonprofit service delivery mechanisms that were designed to make governments better, not emaciated. You don't "reinvent government" with a fiscal meat ax, but by making sure that government pursues only the most effective strategies.

The role of government is to step in where private enterprise cannot. Government provides for its citizens' welfare and security, and manages the conflicting and convergent needs of its people and enterprises. Like a good business manager, government must plan for the future – not just today – by investing for the long term, capitalizing on current strengths, developing potential, and working to surmount liabilities. The challenge is to overcome pressure to provide a quick fix, and instead to work to position the national, state, or local economy so that it is better equipped to handle the economic highs and lows that will inevitably come its way.

If the 1992-93 recovery produced too few jobs, the real question is how do we minimize the possibility of that happening in the future? Government does this by strategically working to make the economy more vital and dynamic, and with better resources upon which to draw, for these are what will help to achieve a strong and healthy economy able to recover from adversity.

Given the tentative national recovery and an increasing debate on the business climate, what really did happen in the last year to the 50 states, individually, regionally, and as a nation, and where are they headed?

The 1994 Report Card Honor Roll

Eight states receive at least two As or Bs, and no grade lower than a C in Economic Performance, Business Vitality, and Development Capacity in the 1994 Report Card. Two of the highest ranking states are in the Mountain West (CO, UT), followed by two in the Northeast (DE, NJ), one in the Pacific (WA), two in the Industrial Midwest (MN, PA), and one from the South (VA).

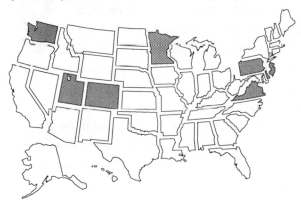

Five states (CO, DE, MN, PA, UT) earn all As and Bs, unlike last year when only Colorado could manage that feat:

- **Colorado:** Colorado has straight As this year, and for the second year receives the best overall grades in the nation. Economic Performance has been increasing steadily from a D in 1991 to an A in 1994. In fact, the only subindexes in which Colorado does not receive an A or B are in the Competitiveness of Existing Business, Earnings & Job Quality,

and Financial Resources. But as a recent Federal Reserve bank regional report notes, there are concerns about how well this can be sustained as other states (particularly in the Midwest) start to catch up.

- **Utah:** Tied with Minnesota for the next highest grades, Utah receives As in Performance and Capacity and a B in Vitality. The state actually ranks second best in the nation in Economic Performance, and first in employment. Interestingly, Utah's weaknesses mirror Colorado's, only they are worse, as it receives Ds in Competitiveness of Existing Business and Financial Resources. But, unlike Colorado, Utah maintains a B in Earnings & Job Quality. The state's upturn in Business Vitality after two years of decline, while still maintaining As in Economic Performance and Development Capacity, bodes well for the future.

- **Minnesota:** Like Utah, Minnesota has As in Performance and Capacity and a B in Vitality, similar to its 1991 and 1992 Report Card grades. For the second year in a row, Minnesota has the best ranking in Development Capacity, due mostly to its high financial and human resources and its strong infrastructure and amenities. Its businesses are competitive (6th in the nation) and it ranks in the top twenty in all three Economic Performance subindexes. With its history of strong civic involvement, and excellent resources, it is not surprising that Minnesota is bouncing back from two Cs last year towards the head of the class again.

- **Delaware:** Delaware receives straight Bs this year, after a pair of As in Economic Performance and Development Capacity accompanied by a D in Vitality last year. This small state is susceptible to many outside forces as shown by its 47th place rank in Structural Diversity, but manages to rate second best in Competitiveness of Existing Business. As long as nothing threatens the state's key sectors, it should remain near the top as it has the past five years.

- **Pennsylvania:** Pennsylvania also earns straight Bs, as Economic Performance improved from a C last year and Vitality and Development Capacity held steady. Good structural diversity, strong earnings and job quality, and financial resources have helped Pennsylvania stay competitive, although it is one of the worst in entrepreneurial energy. The state has the resources and the energy to continue moving forward but it will require hard work.

And although no one likes to focus on the bad news, the poor performance of a couple of states needs to be mentioned:

- **California:** Once a contender, California is now reeling. Last year it received two Cs and an A (the latter in Development Capacity), but in 1994 Development Capacity slips to a B and, worst of all, Performance plummets to an F. Not only does California score poorly in Employment (a D), but it places last in Equity. Only Earnings & Job Quality is okay, ranking 24th in the nation, but the average annual pay figures are from 1992 and may have continued to fall in 1993. Defense cutbacks, riots, earthquakes, and duplicative regulation requirements are still taking their toll.

- **West Virginia:** After two years of modest improvements, the state falls back to straight Fs, just as in 1991. The good signs are a rank of 15 (a B) in Competitiveness of Existing Business, and a C in Equity. But the state's previous strong showing in Business Vitality has evaporated as entrepreneurship, which was strong last year (a B) falls back down to an F due to small change in new companies. The state is making strides, though, particularly in human resources.

What About Taxes?

Looking at how the Report Card's top performers score in the Tax & Fiscal System Index provides a couple of interesting insights. Colorado, Utah, and Minnesota, the top three performing states in the three major Indexes also score well in Tax & Fiscal. Minnesota is the top scoring state in this index for the second year in a row, reflecting a sound and balanced tax system which has no doubt helped it remain perennially near the top of the Report Card ranks for years.

The Mountain West, which includes recent stars Colorado and Utah, has the strongest regional performance in Tax & Fiscal this year, scoring particularly well in both Fiscal Stability & Balanced Revenue and Fiscal Equalization. Meanwhile, the region has also been slowly improving towards the upper Report Card grades these past few years.

The Northeast as a region performs worst in Tax & Fiscal, with only Maine scoring in the top fifteen. The region is particularly weak in Fiscal Equalization which measures how much a state attempts to compensate for local tax differentials (mostly property-based) causing great variation in basic public services, particularly education. Given the region's especially difficult urban problems, which are heavily affected in the long run by education and public welfare, this may not be smart and may further hamper the region's attempts to climb back to the top.

Changes

The Industrial Midwest is the "Comeback Kid." In 1993, we noticed the region was "like a boxer struggling to his knees after a hard blow." Today, with the exception of Missouri, the Midwest is up and swinging. Half of the states score an A or B in Economic Performance. Job growth has been modest, but midwesterners are getting better pay with good benefits and suffer less from poverty and unemployment. In fact, the Midwest is home to three of only five states in the country where job quality and job quantity are both high, and where income disparity is low. How did they pull it off? Yes, a lot of unemployed people migrated south or west, or left the job market altogether, but the economy did recover in its own right. After two decades of painful retrenchment and layoffs, the region seems to have bottomed out. Business closings have come to a near halt, and the newly restructured traditional industries have started to compete globally. The region has also managed to dodge the bullet on the defense build-down. Only Missouri's economy is significantly dependent on both defense spending and defense employment.

A few individual states experienced very large index grade changes. Alaska, Indiana, Minnesota, and New Hampshire all improved by two or more grades in Economic Performance while Maryland, Missouri, and California dropped at least two grades in the past year. Arkansas, South Dakota, and West Virginia declined precipitously in Business Vitality, while Delaware, Indiana, Missouri, and New Jersey all posted strong improvements. As might be expected, not a single state moved more than one grade in either direction in Development Capacity.

Looking ahead, some states bear close watching. Illinois and North Dakota could be big movers in the next few years. Although both states receive Ds in Economic Performance for the second year in a row, both also posted marked gains in Business Vitality and Development Capacity (Illinois moving up from Bs to As and North Dakota from a C to B in Business Vitality; D to C in Development Capacity). With these improvements in economic resources and energy, both states have the prerequisites to earn strong future Economic Performance grades.

Meanwhile, New Jersey should provide a very interesting study. Despite its negative characterization in the recent gubernatorial campaign, the state actually performed very well this past year. Business Vitality jumped from a C

to an A and Development Capacity improved from a B to an A over 1991-1993. The new governor has promised a change in direction. Whether this will positively impact Economic Performance (a steady C), or lead to a decline, remains to be seen.

South Dakota will also bear watching: it is the worst ranking state in the Tax & Fiscal System Index, illustrating how limited state maneuverability is, although the growth of Citibank's credit services has had a positive impact. Finally, two of the Pacific's leaders, Oregon and Washington, may be putting themselves in precarious fiscal positions. Both states score poorly in Tax & Fiscal, echoing concerns raised by Paul Sommers and John Mitchell in *Northwest Portrait 1994* that recent tax actions "have made fiscal uncertainty the order of the day." In fact, three of the five Pacific states, including Oregon and Washington, are in the bottom ten in fiscal stability and balanced revenue. The Pacific may find itself less able to respond to future problems and opportunities.

The Class Of 1990 – Where Are They Now?

In 1990 the New England and Mid-Atlantic states were a powerful group. Led by Connecticut, Maryland, Massachusetts, New Jersey, Pennsylvania, and Vermont (who received all As and Bs), and accompanied by Delaware, New Hampshire, and New York (with two As/Bs and one C), this region was reaping the benefits of the roaring 1980s. These states were among the most severely hit by the recent recession, and although they are now bouncing back, they have not yet been able to overtake the Pacific and Mountain West.

The poorest performers overall in 1990 were Oklahoma, North Dakota, West Virginia, and Louisiana who all rated straight Ds and Fs. Only North Dakota has now distanced itself from the other states, earning a B in Vitality, and a C in Capacity, though it still gets a D in Performance.

The 1994 Development Report Card

9

1990 Development Capacity Compared to 1994 Economic Performance

State	1990 Development Capacity Rank	1990 Development Capacity Grade	1994 Economic Performance Grade
Minnesota	1	A	A
Connecticut	2	A	B
Massachusetts	3	A	C
Washington	4	A	B
Colorado	5	A	A
New Jersey	6	A	C
Delaware	7	A	B
Utah	8	A	A
Oregon	9	A	B
Maryland	10	A	C
Pennsylvania	10	A	B

The stars in Development Capacity a few years ago are doing very well as a group in Economic Performance this year. Of the 11 states receiving an A (there was a tie) in Development Capacity in 1990, three now have an A in Economic Performance – Colorado, Minnesota and Utah, and they have the best overall grades this year. Of that 11 in 1990, another five have a B in Economic Performance this year (CT, DE, OR, PA, and WA); three receive Cs (MD, MA, and NJ). None of these 1990 stars receive a D or F.

1994 Economic Performance Grades for the Top 11 States in 1990 Development Capacity

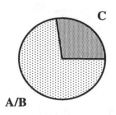

☐ A/B ▨ C

73% of all 11 states with As in Development Capacity in 1990 got an A or B in Economic Performance in 1994, and none got a D or F.

1994 Economic Performance Grades for the Bottom 10 States in 1990 Development Capacity

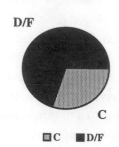

▨ C ■ D/F

70% of the ten worst-ranked states in Development Capacity in 1990 got a D or F in Economic Performance in 1994.

Lessons

Some other conclusions can be drawn from the 1994 Report Card. They do not apply to all cases, as every state is unique, but they do pose some interesting questions for further study.

Economies with good foundations perform the best.
Year after year, the Report Card graphically demonstrates that a state's Economic Performance is highly correlated to its past investments in Development Capacity – their human, financial, technological, and infrastructure resources. The Class of 1990 illustrates this well: of the top eleven in Development Capacity, all but three (73%) receive an A or B in Economic Performance four years later, and none receive Ds or Fs. The reverse is true for the bottom ten states in 1990 Development Capacity; all but three states receive a D or F in 1994 Economic Performance, and none have As or Bs.

Unfortunately, it takes a long time to simmer these ingredients into a healthy economic stew – perhaps a generation or more – so many states recruit investment as a quick way to secure job and earnings growth. Like fast food delivered to the door, recruitment brings immediate relief to the local economies that receive them, yet may not always be the best diet for a long and healthy life.

The Corporation for Enterprise Development

Recruitment is a necessary tool in a state's development arsenal, but unless recruitment is part of a larger, long-term strategy that also develops the resources and infrastructure businesses need to stay competitive, results often don't last. North Carolina is perhaps the best recruiter in the country, but this fact could not save it from slipping a grade in Economic Performance from a B to a C. While a strong Development Capacity will not guarantee economic success, states with a history of balanced investment in their Development Capacity possess the internal strength and flexibility to face global competition and weather bad economic times.

High-technology states have better jobs.

The American economy is the envy of the world for the number of jobs it has created – two million in the past year alone. But being on a payroll doesn't guarantee economic security any more. Some of the fastest growing job markets, such as Idaho, South Carolina, and Arizona, tend to offer less in the way of pay and benefits. Only a handful of states with excellent job growth rate well in the Earnings & Job Quality Subindex (HI, IN, MN, NV, OR, VT, and WI). What can states do to boost the earning power of a greater share of their workforce? States with the best average pay growth and benefits are generally those with the best access to technology and capital resources. Venture capital investments and college graduates, for instance, seem strongly associated with pay growth and health coverage. Not all jobs are created equal, and if a state's primary need is more "good" jobs at "good" wages then the focus should be on increasing use of capital and technology.

**Good Technology Resources
Go Hand in Hand with Good
Jobs**

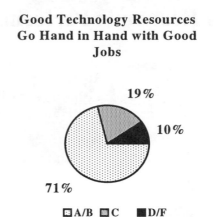

Fifteen of the twenty-one states receiving an A or B in Technology Resources in 1994 also get an A or B in Earnings & Job Quality.

The concern, of course, is that increasing modernization, while improving productivity, lowers employment. Technology often leads to more better-made products, produced by fewer people. It is a fine balancing act between current needs and future possibilities.

1994 Economic Performance Index

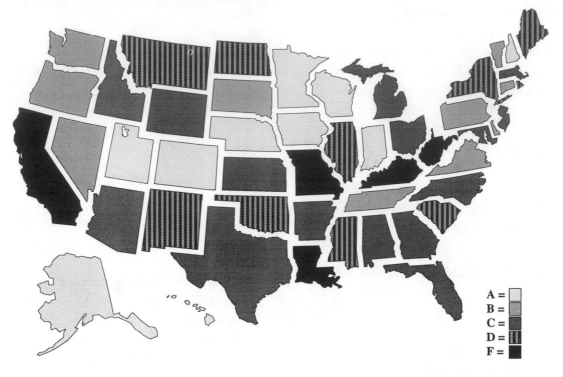

A =
B =
C =
D =
F =

Economic Performance: *How many economic benefits and opportunities for growth is the state economy providing its populace?* The bottom line on how an economy is doing, and an indicator of whether a state offers a good place for businesses to grow, is a state's current performance – that is, how well it does its job of providing citizens opportunities for employment, earnings, and widely shared growth.

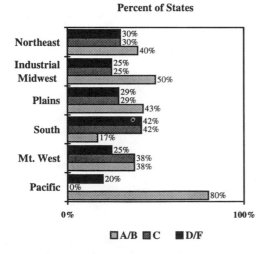

Percent of States

Northeast: 30%, 30%, 40%
Industrial Midwest: 25%, 25%, 50%
Plains: 29%, 29%, 43%
South: 42%, 42%, 17%
Mt. West: 25%, 38%, 38%
Pacific: 0%, 20%, 80%

0%   100%

▨ A/B ▨ C ■ D/F

- The Pacific Coast continues to lead the nation in Economic Performance, with 80% of the region's states earning an A or B. In hot pursuit is the resurgent Industrial Midwest, in which this year half of the states received an A or B on Economic Performance.

- In the middle of the group, with grades fairly evenly spread, are the Northeast, the Plains, and the Mountain West. All three have slipped somewhat since last year – both the Plains and the Mountain West have fewer As and Bs compared with last year, and the Northeast has more Ds and Fs.

- Faring least well in Economic Performance is the South, with only 17% of its states receiving an A or B. Although this figure is below last year's, the South also has fewer states that receive a D or F, indicating a movement in the South towards C-range grades.

The Corporation for Enterprise Development

1994 Economic Performance Report Card

Overall Index			Employment Subindex		Earnings & Job Quality Subindex		Equity Subindex	
Grade	Rank		Rank	Grade	Rank	Grade	Rank	Grade
A	1	Hawaii	4	A	3	A	9	A
	2	Utah	1	A	16	B	3	A
	3	Wisconsin	5	A	11	B	6	A
	4	Iowa	2	A	21	C	1	A
	5	Indiana	6	A	20	B	15	B
	6	Colorado	7	A	27	C	8	A
	6	Minnesota	17	B	13	B	12	B
	8	Nebraska	7	A	34	C	2	A
	9	Alaska	11	B	33	C	5	A
	10	New Hampshire	36	D	9	A	7	A
B	11	Delaware	21	C	19	B	14	B
	11	Virginia	22	C	21	C	11	B
	13	Washington	24	C	7	A	25	C
	14	Oregon	12	B	16	B	30	C
	15	Connecticut	45	D	1	A	13	B
	16	Vermont	23	C	24	C	17	B
	17	Nevada	14	B	15	B	38	D
	17	Pennsylvania	39	D	5	A	23	C
	19	South Dakota	16	B	43	D	10	A
	19	Tennessee	10	A	21	C	38	D
C	21	Arkansas	19	B	37	D	15	B
	22	Wyoming	31	C	41	D	4	A
	22	North Carolina	15	B	28	C	33	C
	24	New Jersey	48	F	2	A	27	C
	25	Florida	20	B	36	D	22	C
	25	Ohio	37	D	10	A	31	C
	27	Texas	25	C	24	C	32	C
	28	Alabama	32	C	30	C	21	C
	28	Arizona	9	A	39	D	35	C
	28	Kansas	26	C	32	C	25	C
	31	Idaho	3	A	40	D	41	D
	32	Georgia	12	B	29	C	44	D
	32	Maryland	34	C	16	B	35	C
	32	Michigan	29	C	11	B	45	D
	35	Massachusetts	41	D	4	A	42	D
D	36	New York	47	F	6	A	38	D
	36	North Dakota	28	C	45	D	18	B
	38	Montana	30	C	47	F	18	B
	39	Rhode Island	50	F	13	B	35	C
	40	Illinois	44	D	8	A	47	F
	41	South Carolina	34	C	42	D	27	C
	42	Maine	48	F	38	D	20	B
	43	New Mexico	27	C	48	F	34	C
	44	Mississippi	17	B	48	F	46	F
	44	Oklahoma	38	D	50	F	23	C
F	46	Kentucky	33	C	31	C	48	F
	47	California	42	D	24	C	50	F
	47	West Virginia	43	D	44	D	29	C
	49	Missouri	40	D	35	C	49	F
	50	Louisiana	46	F	45	D	42	D

1994 Business Vitality Index

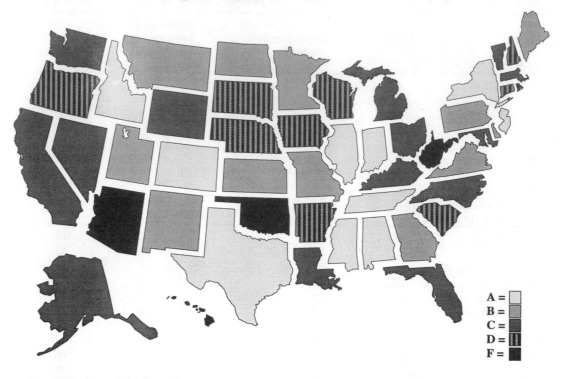

A =
B =
C =
D =
F =

Business Vitality: *How vital is the state's business sector?* The vitality of any state economy is determined by the strength and dynamism of the businesses located there – that is, how competitive they are, how diversified, and how many new ones are being created each year.

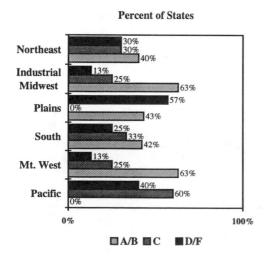

Percent of States

Northeast	30% / 30% / 40%	
Industrial Midwest	13% / 25% / 63%	
Plains	57% / 0% / 43%	
South	25% / 33% / 42%	
Mt. West	13% / 25% / 63%	
Pacific	40% / 60% / 0%	

0%   100%

◼ A/B ◼ C ◼ D/F

- The Mountain West and the Industrial Midwest lead the nation in Business Vitality – in both regions 63% of the states receive an A or B, and both have only one state with a D or F. While the grades from the Mountain West repeat those of last year, the Industrial Midwest's results represent a marked improvement from last year's grades.

- The Plains and the South also do fairly well in Business Vitality – in both regions, slightly less than half of the states receive an A or B. The South's performance represents a drop from last year, when the region led the nation. The Plains' performance is a mixed blessing – more As and Bs than last year, but also more Ds and Fs.

- As was the case last year, the Pacific Coast, despite its strong economic performance, is at the bottom in Business Vitality. Due in large part to poorly diversified economies, no state receives an A or B, and 40% of the states receive a D or F.

1994 Business Vitality Report Card

Overall Index			Competitiveness of Existing Business Subindex		Entrepreneurial Energy Subindex		Structural Diversity Subindex	
Grade	Rank		Rank	Grade	Rank	Grade	Rank	Grade
A	1	Texas	17	B	10	A	4	A
	2	Indiana	1	A	31	C	12	B
	3	Colorado	29	C	14	B	2	A
	3	New Jersey	4	A	9	A	32	C
	5	Tennessee	10	A	29	C	9	A
	6	Alabama	9	A	28	C	14	B
	6	Illinois	12	B	30	C	9	A
	8	Mississippi	24	C	23	C	5	A
	9	New York	11	B	13	B	29	C
	10	Idaho	7	A	4	A	44	D
B	11	Delaware	2	A	11	B	47	F
	11	Georgia	22	C	25	C	13	B
	11	New Mexico	47	F	6	A	7	A
	14	Montana	35	C	7	A	22	C
	15	Utah	42	D	3	A	20	B
	16	Kansas	34	C	16	B	16	B
	17	Maine	33	C	19	B	15	B
	17	Minnesota	6	A	43	D	18	B
	19	North Dakota	3	A	45	D	22	C
	20	Missouri	49	F	14	B	8	A
	20	Pennsylvania	18	B	50	F	3	A
	20	Virginia	46	F	24	C	1	A
C	23	Vermont	37	D	8	A	28	C
	24	Kentucky	23	C	45	D	6	A
	24	Washington	27	C	1	A	46	F
	26	Alaska	26	C	2	A	48	F
	26	North Carolina	32	C	27	C	17	B
	28	Maryland	44	D	22	C	11	B
	29	Ohio	12	B	48	F	19	B
	30	Massachusetts	7	A	44	D	29	C
	30	Nevada	14	B	16	B	50	F
	32	Florida	50	F	5	A	26	C
	32	Michigan	5	A	41	D	35	C
	34	Louisiana	28	C	19	B	35	C
	35	California	37	D	26	C	25	C
	35	Wyoming	16	B	38	D	34	C
D	37	Wisconsin	21	C	39	D	29	C
	38	Iowa	36	D	34	C	20	B
	39	Arkansas	24	C	33	C	37	D
	39	New Hampshire	43	D	11	B	40	D
	39	Oregon	40	D	16	B	38	D
	39	South Dakota	20	B	31	C	43	D
	43	Connecticut	19	B	36	D	42	D
	44	Nebraska	30	C	35	C	33	C
	45	South Carolina	30	C	49	F	22	C
F	46	West Virginia	15	B	47	F	44	D
	47	Oklahoma	41	D	40	D	26	C
	48	Hawaii	44	D	21	C	48	F
	49	Rhode Island	37	D	41	D	39	D
	50	Arizona	47	F	36	D	41	D

1994 Development Capacity Index

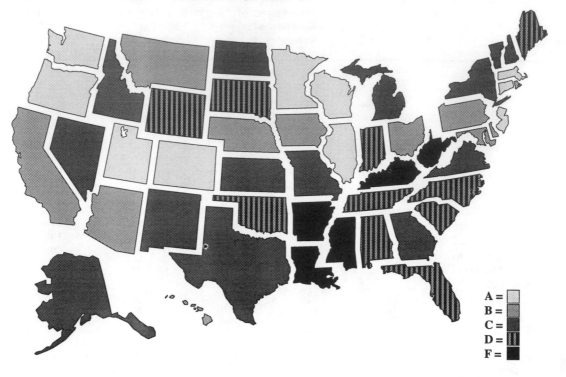

A =
B =
C =
D =
F =

Development Capacity: *What is the state's capacity for continued growth and recovery from economic adversity?* The future of both today's and tomorrow's businesses is tied directly to the quality and availability of the "building blocks" of economies – a skilled workforce, technology resources, financial resources, and physical infrastructure and amenity resources.

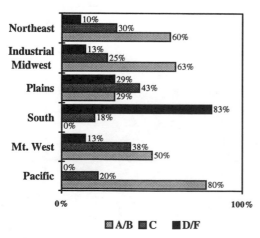

Percent of States

- As it did last year, the Pacific Coast leads the nation in Development Capacity, with 80% of the region's states receiving an A or B. Not far behind are the Industrial Midwest and the Northeast, with roughly 60% of states receiving As or Bs.

- The Plains region shows strong improvement from last year, with twice as many As and Bs and half as many Ds and Fs. Yet, the region's overall lackluster results in Development Capacity reflect relatively weak financial and technology resources.

- Poor to begin with, the South's Development Capacity grades dropped slightly from last year as the region lost its only A/B performer (Virginia). Scarred by its poor human resources, 83% of the states in the region score a D or F in Development Capacity – the worst single performance by any region on any index.

1994 Development Capacity Report Card

Overall Index			Human Resources Subindex		Technology Resources Subindex		Financial Resources Subindex		Infrastructure & Amenity Resources Subindex	
Grade	Rank		Rank	Grade	Rank	Grade	Rank	Grade	Rank	Grade
A	1	Minnesota	5	A	20	B	3	A	2	A
	2	Colorado	4	A	3	A	34	C	1	A
	3	Washington	9	A	16	B	14	B	8	A
	4	Massachusetts	2	A	1	A	2	A	45	D
	4	Utah	5	A	4	A	38	D	3	A
	6	Illinois	17	B	20	B	4	A	10	A
	7	Wisconsin	14	B	24	C	16	B	12	B
	8	New Jersey	7	A	13	B	10	A	38	D
	9	Connecticut	1	A	7	A	22	C	39	D
	10	Oregon	22	C	22	C	8	A	19	B
B	11	Delaware	35	C	10	A	12	B	17	B
	11	Maryland	19	B	4	A	29	C	22	C
	13	Hawaii	10	A	23	C	15	B	28	C
	14	Montana	12	B	33	C	32	C	4	A
	15	Pennsylvania	30	C	13	B	6	A	33	C
	16	Nebraska	8	A	36	D	33	C	9	A
	17	Ohio	34	C	16	B	13	B	24	C
	18	Arizona	18	B	15	B	43	D	12	B
	18	Iowa	19	B	28	C	34	C	7	A
	20	California	26	C	9	A	19	B	36	D
	20	Rhode Island	33	C	6	A	1	A	50	F
C	22	Virginia	24	C	11	B	26	C	30	C
	23	Georgia	40	D	39	D	7	A	6	A
	24	New York	36	D	8	A	9	A	42	D
	25	Alaska	16	B	27	C	43	D	15	B
	26	Vermont	11	B	19	B	31	C	41	D
	27	Idaho	25	C	26	C	28	C	24	C
	27	Texas	39	D	25	C	25	C	14	B
	29	Kansas	2	A	42	D	37	D	23	C
	30	Michigan	37	D	18	B	10	A	40	D
	30	North Dakota	19	B	28	C	42	D	16	B
	32	Nevada	23	C	36	D	46	F	5	A
	33	New Hampshire	13	B	12	B	39	D	48	F
	34	Missouri	29	C	32	C	27	C	27	C
	35	New Mexico	30	C	2	A	50	F	35	C
D	36	Florida	37	D	40	D	23	C	18	B
	37	North Carolina	44	D	31	C	5	A	44	D
	37	Wyoming	14	B	34	C	45	D	31	C
	39	Tennessee	46	F	34	C	24	C	21	C
	40	South Dakota	28	C	48	F	18	B	32	C
	41	Alabama	47	F	30	C	17	B	37	D
	42	Oklahoma	32	C	38	D	40	D	24	C
	43	Indiana	41	D	41	D	21	C	33	C
	44	Maine	27	C	46	F	20	B	47	F
	45	South Carolina	47	F	44	D	40	D	11	B
F	46	Kentucky	45	D	49	F	30	C	19	B
	47	Arkansas	42	D	50	F	48	F	29	C
	48	West Virginia	43	D	47	F	36	D	46	F
	49	Louisiana	49	F	43	D	47	F	43	D
	50	Mississippi	50	F	45	D	49	F	49	F

Regional Findings

The following is a regional listing of states and state abbreviations found in the *1994 Development Report Card for the States*.

The Northeast

Connecticut	CT
Delaware	DE
Maine	ME
Maryland	MD
Massachusetts	MA
New Hampshire	NH
New Jersey	NJ
New York	NY
Rhode Island	RI
Vermont	VT

The Industrial Midwest

Illinois	IL
Indiana	IN
Michigan	MI
Minnesota	MN
Missouri	MO
Ohio	OH
Pennsylvania	PA
Wisconsin	WI

The Plains

Iowa	IA
Kansas	KS
Nebraska	NE
North Dakota	ND
Oklahoma	OK
South Dakota	SD
Texas	TX

The South

Alabama	AL
Arkansas	AR
Florida	FL
Georgia	GA
Kentucky	KY
Louisiana	LA
Mississippi	MS
North Carolina	NC
South Carolina	SC
Tennessee	TN
Virginia	VA
West Virginia	WV

The Mountain West

Arizona	AZ
Colorado	CO
Idaho	ID
Montana	MT
Nevada	NV
New Mexico	NM
Utah	UT
Wyoming	WY

The Pacific

Alaska	AK
California	CA
Hawaii	HI
Oregon	OR
Washington	WA

The Northeast

After a poor showing last year, the Northeast's 1994 grades are mixed. In spite of having one of the poorest post-recession job markets in the country, four states (CT, DE, NH, and VT) receive an A or B in Economic Performance with Maine, New York, and Rhode Island lagging behind in the bottom ten. As a region, Northeast jobs pay well and offer better benefits than others around the country, the legacy of the region's traditional strengths in high technology and human resources. The region is also showing strong signs of new business vitality, though not in all states. But the prolonged economic hardships may blemish the Northeast's good record in income distribution, as virtually every state experienced an increase in the income gap between the richest and poorest fifths of the population. No one can coast along on old successes and investments here.

Economic Performance:

- In the late 1980s and early 1990s, the Northeast was the very definition of economic excellence. Virtually all the As in Economic Performance went to the Northeast (plus the two big tourism states – HI and NV). This year only New Hampshire earns an A, and 60% of the Northeast is a C or lower, continuing last year's disappointing performance.

- The Northeast fell hardest in the recent recession and job growth has still not recovered. Seven states earn Ds or Fs, and the remaining three only Cs in Employment. The good news is that the jobs which remain are still among the best; eight states have As or Bs in Earnings & Job Quality (CT, DE, MD, MA, NH, NJ, NY, and RI). Only Maine performs poorly in this category.

- Defense-dependent Maryland performed poorly this year as employment and pay growth came to a complete halt. Unemployment and poverty rates skyrocketed, and the state tumbled two grades in Economic Performance from an A to a C. New Jersey still ranks at the bottom in long- and short-term employment growth, but retains its second-place ranking in Earnings & Job Quality.

A =
B =
C =
D =
F =

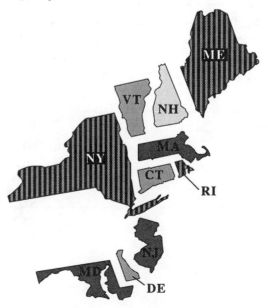

Business Vitality:

- For the second year in a row, the Northeast has mixed scores in Business Vitality. While half the states receive an A or B in Competitiveness of Existing Business, the Northeast has poor sectoral diversity, which will worsen as cutbacks in defense continue to reverberate. Interestingly, entrepreneurship is high. It may be the entrepreneurship of necessity though, as employment growth is low and people are forced to start their own business because they cannot find salaried jobs.

- Rhode Island and New Hampshire's economies may be in trouble down the road. They are among the four states in the country where young companies reduced employment and they have one of the worst records in new manufacturing investment. Nevertheless, New Hampshire is number three in the country for venture capital investments and Rhode Island, eleven.

- The region has stopped losing businesses, and Maine, Massachusetts, and Rhode Island now rank among the 15 best in terms of business closings (last year MA and RI were among the worst).

Development Capacity:

- The Northeast still claims good development capacity. Six of the ten states receive an A or B – though this is down from the region's eight As and Bs in 1990 and 1991. Overall financial and human resources are excellent with only one state scoring poorly in each subindex (NH in Financial Resources and NY in Human Resources). The Northeast is still the high-tech leader of the U.S. as every state but Maine receives As or Bs; in fact, half of the nation's technology As are in the Northeast, including number one ranked Massachusetts.

- Again, infrastructure is this region's Development Capacity weakness, as every state but Delaware and Maryland receives a D or F. Energy costs remain high, bridge deficiency is widespread with every state except Delaware ranking in the bottom half (including the two worst in the country, MA and NY), and sewage treatment needs are pressing. In fact, five of the six lowest ranking states for sewage treatment needs in the country are located in the Northeast.

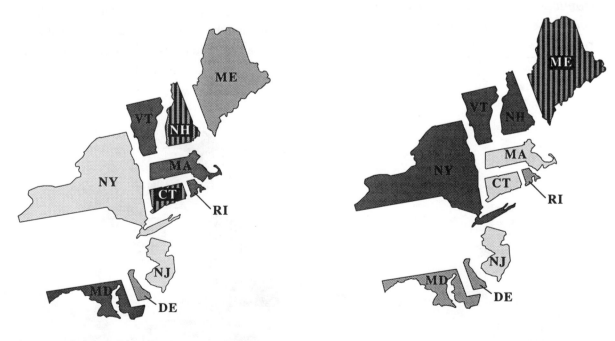

The Industrial Midwest

The industrial heartland is staging a comeback. Six of the eight states improved at least one grade on one or more indexes, and only one (MO) fell in Economic Performance from last year. Average performers in 1990, now half of the Industrial Midwest has an A or B in Economic Performance, and the region as a whole ranks very well in industrial diversity and business competitiveness. After a generation of decline and restructuring, the region is building off its manufacturing base, which is also providing it with a solid record in pay, pay growth, and benefits, and the story doesn't revolve just around autos. Minnesota, for example, is a manufacturing powerhouse. There is just a hint that the new industrialized economy in the Midwest, as elsewhere, is offering fewer low-skill entry-level jobs. The economic growth in the Midwest has been accompanied by an increase in income disparity.

Economic Performance:

- Half the region has As or Bs in the overall Economic Performance Index while three states (IN, MN, and WI) actually score an A or B in all three subindexes: Employment, Earnings & Job Quality, and Equity. Although there has been concern recently that in today's economy pay levels and job growth are almost inversely related, and that equity is affected by little but education, a third of the Midwest bucked this trend.

- Minnesota may be the star of the region, but Pennsylvania deserves an honorable mention. Although the Federal Reserve Bank gives the state mixed reviews on employment prospects, Pennsylvania's pay levels and pay growth remain among the best in the nation, consistent with the state's history of strong investment in technology and capital access.

- Missouri dropped three grades in Economic Performance, no longer competitive in autos and leather products, over-dependent on defense spending (McDonnell Douglas Corporation cut 10,000 jobs in St. Louis), and with a deteriorating record on income disparity. However, Missouri will be an integral part of the region's comeback – major services are moving their headquarters to St. Louis and the big three domestic auto makers have announced plans to renovate and expand production at their St. Louis auto plants.

A =
B =
C =
D =
F =

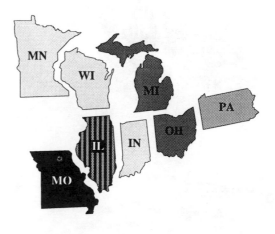

The Corporation for Enterprise Development

Business Vitality:

- The Midwest did very well in Business Vitality: five of eight states (63%) receive an A or B (IL, IN, MN, MO, and PA). This is due to strong grades in both the Competitiveness of Existing Business and Structural Diversity subindexes, in which over 70% of the Midwest score A or B.

- The Midwest's weakness appears in entrepreneurship, where only Missouri managed better than a C and MI, MN, OH, PA, and WI all received a D or F. Business failures finally bottomed out in the middle of 1993 as the country was struggling to pull out of the recession, but the Midwest has had little entrepreneurial activity. It was the region's old regulars that endured, restructured, and got back into the game. Entrepreneurship may rise again soon though as venture capital investments in 1993 were relatively high in half the states (IL, IN, MN, and PA).

Development Capacity:

- Only the Pacific did better than the Midwest here as five of eight Midwest states (63%) score an A or B in Development Capacity (IL, MN, OH, PA, and WI). Illinois improved from a B to an A, and not one state fell. The region is often noted for its solid workforce but interestingly, the Midwest was a financial leader this year. Seventy-five percent of the states receive an A or B in Financial Resources, led by high deposits per capita, loans to deposits, loans to equity, and venture capital investments. Only Missouri is below the median in financial capacity. Technology resources were also very good with Bs for Illinois, Michigan, Minnesota, Ohio, and Pennsylvania – although the latter three all fell a grade from last year in this subindex.

- Indiana and Missouri rank very low in most measures of Development Capacity. Missouri shares the same economic fate of the least endowed of its cousins to the South, but Indiana, also a close cultural kin to the South, is extremely successful. What separates Indiana is a good concentration of highly skilled and experienced production workers, and above-average venture capital activity.

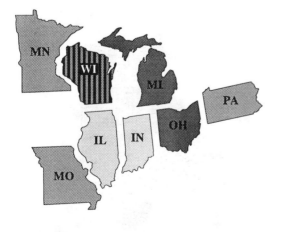

The Plains

The Plains appear to have a split personality. The upper Plains are ultra-small, quiet economies driven by agriculture and services; their very low unemployment rates and good records for income distribution are a reflection of their isolation and industrial restructuring during the 1980s. With a good base of high school-educated workers, low pay, and low taxes, parts of the region have become meccas for credit card processing, tourism, and other services. Meanwhile, three-quarters of the Plains population live in Oklahoma and Texas, two states which have some of the nation's worst records in poverty and income disparity. Texas, however, appears to have made significant progress in diversifying from its oil industry – it ranks as one of the most economically vital and diverse states in the region and country.

Economic Performance:

- Can a state have strong job growth *and* well-paying jobs? Not if you look at the Plains states. The three As and Bs in Employment are paired with Cs and Ds in Earnings & Job Quality in Iowa, Nebraska, and South Dakota. Meanwhile, Kansas and Texas have straight Cs across the subindexes.

- Low-tax South Dakota may look like business heaven, but the state's manufacturing employment base remains small. Although employment growth in the early 1990s has shown improvement, the state ranks 40th in long-term growth, and has little entrepreneurial activity. Citibank and other finance companies are the biggest employers in Sioux Falls, but the locus of the activity is entirely external to the economy.

- Iowa and Nebraska earned the region's only As in Economic Performance, both enjoying particularly strong short-term employment growth, and As in equity. Iowa's economy has been improving for a longer period, partly due to progress in business diversification and the region's best record in pay growth.

A =
B =
C =
D =
F =

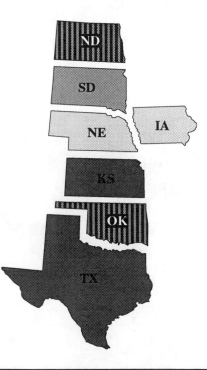

The Corporation for Enterprise Development

Business Vitality:

- Texas adds the spice to the Plains' economy. Texas' high rate of business closings may actually be a healthy sign of restructuring when coupled with its high rates of venture capital activity and new manufacturing investment. Texas' growth is broad-based and future-oriented. It is also sustained – Texas has earned an A in Business Vitality for the third year in a row, up from Cs in the past.

- North Dakota and Kansas deserve honorable mentions. Tourism and new manufacturing investment are breathing new life into North Dakota and both states are enjoying faster-than-average growth in new company formation.

- For the rest of the region, Business Vitality is poor as Iowa, Nebraska, Oklahoma, and South Dakota all earn Ds and Fs. South Dakota plummeted from a B to a D as entrepreneurship fell from seventh to thirty-first.

Development Capacity:

- Second only to the South in the lowest percentage of As and Bs in Development Capacity, only two states out of seven (IA and NE) earn above a C. Nevertheless, this is an improvement over last year in which all states except Texas scored a C or lower.

- Over half the Plains states earn an A or B in Human Resources and Infrastructure, the region's two Development Capacity strengths. They are weakest in financial and technological resources where they can only manage Fs, Ds, a couple of Cs, and one B (for SD in financial resources, which reflects Citibank's credit card services).

- Half of the top ten states for high school graduation are located in the Plains, but these graduates may be leaving or non-graduates may be coming in as high school attainment is mixed with four states (ND, OK, SD, and TX) below the U.S. median.

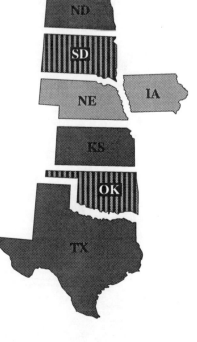

The South

> *The South's overall low grades reflect its history of poor education and low-wage branch industrial plants. The region has a reputation as a job creation powerhouse – six states have an A or B in Employment, and only West Virginia gets below a C. But it is also the land of the working poor – millions of Southerners live two paychecks away from welfare. Thus, many southern states rank near the bottom in measures of pay, health coverage, poverty, and income distribution. Nevertheless, the situation may not be quite so grim. Half the states are in the top half in terms of pay growth, and the South has made true progress in reducing income disparity. Although last year's stellar Business Vitality grades have not been sustained, neither have they fallen back to earlier levels. Despite its legacy, the South is making improvements, just slowly.*

Economic Performance:

- Over the past five years, only Virginia – closely tied to the lower Northeast – has received an A in Economic Performance (in 1993). This year only two states score better than C. Nevertheless, the South continues to have strong job growth as half the states get an A or B in the Employment Subindex. Some states have cooled off a bit, including Alabama, North Carolina, South Carolina, and Virginia, all of which fell to the bottom half in employment growth between 1992 and 1993.

- Arkansas, Georgia, and Tennessee are the region's star performers in terms of economic opportunity – these three rank in the top half in measures of employment growth, low unemployment, and annual average pay growth.

- The Deep South is gambling on the future. Mississippi, the region's surprise performer, scores a B in the Employment Subindex, and press reports suggest that legalized gambling may be a factor. But Mississippi still gets an F in Equity and in Earnings & Job Quality – although most of their component measures are from slightly earlier periods than employment growth, they still point to a need for better paying jobs. In fact, almost half the South gets a D or F in Equity and Earnings & Job Quality.

A =
B =
C =
D =
F =

Business Vitality:

- Some states in the region took a serious tumble in business vitality this year, pushed off track by higher rates of business closings and lower levels of new business formation. West Virginia fell precipitously in Business Vitality, and seems to have bottomed out in business closings although it is number eight in the nation for new manufacturing capital investments. Arkansas' fall was cushioned by continued growth in new company formation and manufacturing capital investment. Nevertheless, five of twelve states receive an A or B in Business Vitality, including three As (AL, MS, TN), making this the South's strongest index for the second year.

- The southern economy is fairly well diversified, if not very competitive. Its traded sector strength is weak (apparel is not very competitive these days). There is evidence, however, that it may become more competitive as nine states rank in the top half in manufacturing capital investments. Moreover, the region may be better prepared than others to weather the defense cuts – only two of the twelve states (MS and VA) are heavily dependent on defense spending.

Development Capacity:

- This is the South's Achilles heel. Ten out of twelve states receive a D or F in Development Capacity – by far the worst of any region in any index. Is it a coincidence that half of the South also gets a D or F in Earnings & Job Quality? Meanwhile, two of the poorest states in the nation – West Virginia and Arkansas – have managed to raise their high school graduation rates to rank in the top half of the fifty states; both states now rank in the top half of the country in recent employment growth.

- The South's technology resources continue to be relatively scarce and concentrated. Without Northern Virginia near Washington, D.C., Atlanta (GA), the Research Triangle Park (NC), Oak Ridge Laboratory (TN), and the aerospace centers in Florida and Huntsville (AL), the South would have little to show.

- The South, historically a net exporter of capital, invented regional banking to grow and retain significant capital reserves. It may be paying off. Much of the South rises to the top of national indicators for deposits and lending activity. Only the Deep South and West Virginia, still very poor, rank low.

The Mountain West

Although the recession and defense cuts have stalled the Mountain West some this year, the region is evolving towards the upper grades in the Report Card over the past five years, aided by a good foundation of basic education and infrastructure and very high levels of entrepreneurship (half the states get As). Defense and leisure are the pillars of the Mountain West economy. Virtually every state ranks in the top 20 of the nation in tourism spending, and half are dependent on federal spending for defense and university research. Colorado and Utah do the best in the Report Card overall. Although neither is a star performer in business competitiveness (an F and a D respectively), both have diverse economies with high-tech centers that are attracting large amounts of venture capital.

Economic Performance:

- Overall, the results are mixed. Three states earn As or Bs (CO, NV, UT), three earn Cs, and two Ds. Employment growth is steady and the duration of unemployment is not long ; out of eight states, four earn As (AZ, CO, ID, and UT), one receives a B (NV), and none a D or F in the Employment Subindex. Earnings are poor, as five state earn Ds and Fs in this category (AZ, ID, MT, NM, and WY). Like the South, jobs outside the high-tech sectors don't pay well.

- Despite earning a B, one of the most notable declines in recent years was Nevada, which ranked number *one* in the nation for Economic Performance in 1991 and 1992. Nevada has clearly put all its eggs into one basket – gambling and entertainment – and the jobs are good for those who have them, but unemployment is high and the state suffers the nation's worst income disparity. With growing competition in the gambling business, Nevada may have lost its edge. The state no longer makes the top ten in Economic Performance.

A =
B =
C =
D =
F =

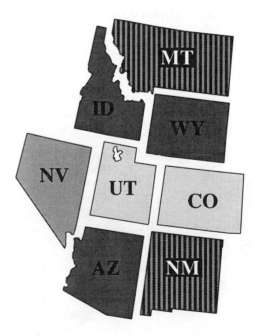

The Corporation for Enterprise Development

Business Vitality:

- Over the past five years, the South and Mountain West stole top honors in this category from the Northeast. This year, the Mountain West ties the Industrial Midwest for top honors in this index, with five of eight states earning an A or B (except AZ, NV, and WY).

- Business failures run high, but the region experienced good rates of new company formation, job growth in young companies, and manufacturing investment, hallmarks of dynamic and growing economies.

- Only Arizona and Utah export above the national average, but Colorado may soon join the ranks. Colorado already has a strong and diverse business structure, and with the recent uptake in venture capital and manufacturing investment, it can be expected to capitalize on NAFTA and its new airport.

- Montana may be the region's surprise in the making. Although it earned an F in Economic Performance, this microbusiness state is number eight in the country for new venture capital per worker, and it earns an A in Entrepreneurial Energy.

Development Capacity:

- The region as a whole is doing well in this index, with its biggest weakness being almost nonexistent financial resources – two Fs, three Ds, and three Cs, and that is it. It has the people (five As and Bs in Human Resources) and the technology (four As and Bs in Technology Resources); now it needs the cash.

- The defense industry has been good to the Mountain West, bringing with it high rates of science and engineering students, research grants, and high-tech investment, making it more than just a nice place to visit and retire.

- Although the border states face huge infrastructure challenges, the region as a whole is quite well off in terms of its physical infrastructure and amenities. Five states earn As or Bs (AZ, CO, MT, NV, and UT) with no Ds or Fs. High energy costs in the non-border states are the biggest negative in the region's development capacity.

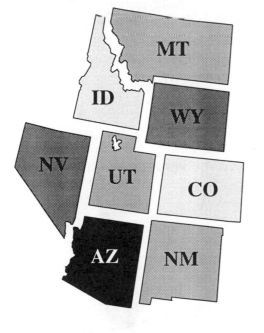

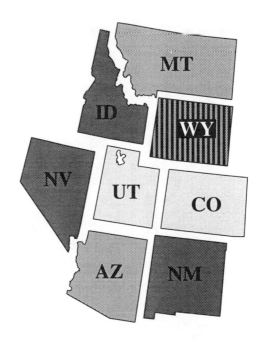

The Pacific

The Pacific, with the exception of Hawaii, is still feeling the punishing blows of economic restructuring and low natural resource prices, and is no longer securely at the top. California is the Pacific disaster area, tumbling two grades in Economic Performance. One of the bright spots is California's intense venture capital activity; those with foresight in the business community are still investing heavily in California's future. Alaska and Hawaii are the stars of the region with top ten economic performances which may be tenuous due to their great lack of diversity. Washington and Oregon, though falling to Bs in Economic Performance, are securing modest gains in employment and pay, helping to mitigate severe contractions in the forest products industry. They have pulled in a surprisingly good amount of new manufacturing investment and even venture capital.

Economic Performance:

- The Pacific is still the Economic Performance leader with all states except California earning As or Bs. This is probably the only region in which many states have good grades in both the Earnings & Job Quality and Employment subindexes. Despite layoffs in aerospace and defense, the region has not suffered as much as might have been expected (only CA earns a failing grade in Employment).

- Over the years, strong economies have left the Pacific with good wage jobs; all but Oregon had average annual wages in the top fifteen. Wages have been growing fast for all but Alaska. Poverty is low in each state except California (affected by immigration), and the disparity between rich and poor is relatively small.

- Alaska and Hawaii, the two most physically isolated states, have the region's best grades in Economic Performance. They are the only two states in this region that managed to decrease the gap between rich and poor from the late 1980s to early 1990s. Hawaii ranks number one in Economic Performance, with strong grades in each subindex (third in Earnings & Job Quality, fourth in Employment, and ninth in Equity).

A =
B =
C =
D =
F =

Business Vitality:

- Overall the region is lackluster in Business Vitality with no states earning As or Bs in Structural Diversity or Competitiveness of Existing Business. Alaska, Hawaii, and Washington receive Fs in Structural Diversity; Oregon manages a D, and California, of all places, leads with a C. Meanwhile, business closings remain high as Alaska, California, Oregon, and Washington all rank among the worst ten in the nation, and manufacturing capital investment was low in all but Oregon and Washington.

- The bright spot is entrepreneurship, as the Pacific struggles to maintain a dynamic business sector. Washington is an entrepreneurial hot spot, ranking number one in the nation for new company formation, followed by Alaska and then California two places back. Job growth (measured for the early 1990s) from young companies was also strong in those states.

Development Capacity:

- The Pacific scores the highest of any region in Development Capacity with California, Hawaii, Oregon, and Washington earning an A or B. Only Alaska earns a C, largely due to a lack of fiscal resources, while Oregon rose from a B to an A, due to its improved Human Resources. California, however, has been so seized by fiscal troubles that it appears to be disinvesting in its Development Capacity, slipping from an A to B.

- The region as a whole has attracted relatively higher proportions of college graduates, but ranks only somewhat better than the South in high school graduation. This could threaten the region's good equity and low income disparity in the future if there is little opportunity for growth and advancement for relatively unskilled workers.

Regional & State Trends: 1990–1994
Economic Performance Index

	1990 Rank	1990 Grade	1991 Rank	1991 Grade	1992 Rank	1992 Grade	1993 Rank	1993 Grade	1994 Rank	1994 Grade
Northeast										
Connecticut	8	A	10	A	8	A	11	B	15	B
Delaware	2	A	6	A	3	A	1	A	11	B
Maine	12	B	7	A	22	C	24	C	42	D
Maryland	6	A	3	A	2	A	5	A	32	C
Massachusetts	4	A	21	C	28	C	34	C	35	C
New Hampshire	1	A	2	A	12	B	21	C	10	A
New Jersey	9	A	5	A	16	B	24	C	24	C
New York	29	C	37	D	34	C	44	D	36	D
Rhode Island	7	A	16	B	20	B	32	C	39	D
Vermont	5	A	17	B	13	B	13	B	16	B
Industrial Midwest										
Illinois	37	D	35	C	26	C	36	D	40	D
Indiana	11	B	22	C	20	B	30	C	5	A
Michigan	31	C	27	C	31	C	40	D	32	C
Minnesota	13	B	18	B	11	B	23	C	6	A
Missouri	29	C	40	D	24	C	18	B	49	F
Ohio	18	B	35	C	25	C	26	C	25	C
Pennsylvania	15	B	13	B	15	B	22	C	17	B
Wisconsin	16	B	9	A	7	A	3	A	3	A
Plains										
Iowa	31	C	23	C	18	B	9	A	4	A
Kansas	21	C	15	B	13	B	17	B	28	C
Nebraska	26	C	12	B	5	A	6	A	8	A
North Dakota	36	D	30	C	37	D	45	D	36	D
Oklahoma	45	D	40	D	46	F	46	F	44	D
South Dakota	42	D	29	C	39	D	20	B	19	B
Texas	41	D	43	D	39	D	29	C	27	C
South										
Alabama	44	D	44	D	41	D	38	D	28	C
Arkansas	43	D	45	D	47	F	19	B	21	C
Florida	17	B	23	C	32	C	30	C	25	C
Georgia	28	C	28	C	30	C	43	D	32	C
Kentucky	47	F	47	F	42	D	50	F	46	F
Louisiana	50	F	50	F	49	F	49	F	50	F
Mississippi	45	D	46	F	50	F	48	F	44	D
North Carolina	21	C	19	B	17	B	14	B	22	C
South Carolina	24	C	23	C	34	C	40	D	41	D
Tennessee	40	D	34	C	38	D	34	C	19	B
Virginia	14	B	19	B	23	C	4	A	11	B
West Virginia	49	F	49	F	44	D	47	F	47	F
Mountain West										
Arizona	23	C	30	C	34	C	42	D	28	C
Colorado	39	D	39	D	33	C	15	B	6	A
Idaho	33	C	33	C	19	B	12	B	31	C
Montana	38	D	48	F	43	D	32	C	38	D
Nevada	10	A	1	A	1	A	15	B	17	B
New Mexico	47	F	40	D	48	F	37	D	43	D
Utah	18	B	13	B	9	A	10	A	2	A
Wyoming	35	C	30	C	27	C	26	C	22	C
Pacific										
Alaska	33	C	37	D	45	D	38	D	9	A
California	18	B	26	C	28	C	28	C	47	F
Hawaii	2	A	3	A	6	A	8	A	1	A
Oregon	25	C	11	B	9	A	6	A	14	B
Washington	26	C	8	A	4	A	2	A	13	B

The Corporation for Enterprise Development

Regional & State Trends: 1990–1994
Business Vitality Index

	1990 Rank	1990 Grade	1991 Rank	1991 Grade	1992 Rank	1992 Grade	1993 Rank	1993 Grade	1994 Rank	1994 Grade
Northeast										
Connecticut	11	B	7	A	15	B	31	C	43	D
Delaware	25	C	19	B	9	A	43	D	11	B
Maine	5	A	17	B	17	B	6	A	17	B
Maryland	9	A	9	A	20	B	28	C	28	C
Massachusetts	12	B	12	B	39	D	20	B	30	C
New Hampshire	1	A	1	A	41	D	46	F	39	D
New Jersey	2	A	5	A	12	B	30	C	3	A
New York	10	A	6	A	24	C	19	B	9	A
Rhode Island	31	C	23	C	35	C	48	F	49	F
Vermont	8	A	21	C	16	B	16	B	23	C
Industrial Midwest										
Illinois	27	C	26	C	17	B	11	B	6	A
Indiana	15	B	30	C	6	A	26	C	2	A
Michigan	35	C	42	D	38	D	28	C	32	C
Minnesota	21	C	4	A	5	A	34	C	17	B
Missouri	33	C	35	C	30	C	40	D	20	B
Ohio	40	D	45	D	30	C	34	C	29	C
Pennsylvania	19	B	15	B	21	C	15	B	20	B
Wisconsin	45	D	40	D	24	C	40	D	37	D
Plains										
Iowa	44	D	41	D	3	A	43	D	38	D
Kansas	37	D	36	D	12	B	34	C	16	B
Nebraska	41	D	32	C	26	C	45	D	44	D
North Dakota	49	F	49	F	26	C	22	C	19	B
Oklahoma	47	F	47	F	45	D	40	D	47	F
South Dakota	35	C	26	C	10	A	20	B	39	D
Texas	34	C	24	C	1	A	1	A	1	A
South										
Alabama	17	B	13	B	23	C	2	A	6	A
Arkansas	23	C	42	D	34	C	5	A	39	D
Florida	19	B	15	B	33	C	37	D	32	C
Georgia	3	A	26	C	46	F	10	A	11	B
Kentucky	15	B	32	C	26	C	13	B	24	C
Louisiana	48	F	50	F	47	F	37	D	34	C
Mississippi	23	C	32	C	37	D	16	B	8	A
North Carolina	5	A	2	A	35	C	13	B	26	C
South Carolina	38	D	38	D	49	F	47	F	45	D
Tennessee	5	A	31	C	29	C	8	A	5	A
Virginia	4	A	11	B	19	B	26	C	20	B
West Virginia	43	D	46	F	42	D	16	B	46	F
Mountain West										
Arizona	26	C	26	C	50	F	49	F	50	F
Colorado	12	B	8	A	3	A	4	A	3	A
Idaho	45	D	36	D	7	A	7	A	10	A
Montana	42	D	39	D	30	C	8	A	14	B
Nevada	29	C	13	B	21	C	31	C	30	C
New Mexico	21	C	17	B	2	A	3	A	11	B
Utah	27	C	10	A	11	B	22	C	15	B
Wyoming	50	F	48	F	43	D	11	B	35	C
Pacific										
Alaska	30	C	20	B	14	B	39	D	26	C
California	14	B	3	A	8	A	25	C	35	C
Hawaii	38	D	44	D	48	F	50	F	48	F
Oregon	17	B	21	C	44	D	22	C	39	D
Washington	32	C	24	C	40	D	33	C	24	C

Regional & State Trends: 1990–1994
Development Capacity Index

	1990		1991		1992		1993		1994	
	Rank	Grade	Rank	Grade	Rank	Grade	Rank	Grade	Rank	Grade
Northeast										
Connecticut	2	A	5	A	12	B	8	A	9	A
Delaware	7	A	7	A	15	B	7	A	11	B
Maine	37	D	43	D	45	D	45	D	44	D
Maryland	10	A	9	A	9	A	6	A	11	B
Massachusetts	3	A	4	A	4	A	5	A	4	A
New Hampshire	22	C	14	B	25	C	30	C	33	C
New Jersey	6	A	10	A	18	B	11	B	8	A
New York	13	B	24	C	7	A	18	B	24	C
Rhode Island	20	B	16	B	23	C	23	C	20	B
Vermont	16	B	20	B	13	B	25	C	26	C
Industrial Midwest										
Illinois	13	B	19	B	11	B	17	B	6	A
Indiana	33	C	36	D	33	C	43	D	43	D
Michigan	29	C	25	C	22	C	31	C	30	C
Minnesota	1	A	1	A	1	A	1	A	1	A
Missouri	33	C	33	C	26	C	34	C	34	C
Ohio	23	C	12	B	17	B	15	B	17	B
Pennsylvania	10	A	10	A	21	C	13	B	15	B
Wisconsin	25	C	31	C	10	A	9	A	7	A
Plains										
Iowa	39	D	35	C	26	C	29	C	18	B
Kansas	36	D	25	C	29	C	32	C	29	C
Nebraska	27	C	25	C	33	C	22	C	16	B
North Dakota	43	D	42	D	46	F	42	D	30	C
Oklahoma	42	D	44	D	44	D	39	D	42	D
South Dakota	32	C	32	C	37	D	44	D	40	D
Texas	17	B	22	C	19	B	20	B	27	C
South										
Alabama	45	D	45	D	43	D	39	D	41	D
Arkansas	48	F	48	F	49	F	47	F	47	F
Florida	41	D	39	D	40	D	36	D	36	D
Georgia	38	D	34	C	31	C	21	C	23	C
Kentucky	47	F	46	F	42	D	46	F	46	F
Louisiana	46	F	47	F	47	F	49	F	49	F
Mississippi	50	F	50	F	50	F	50	F	50	F
North Carolina	24	C	29	C	24	C	37	D	37	D
South Carolina	44	D	41	D	41	D	41	D	45	D
Tennessee	40	D	40	D	26	C	37	D	39	D
Virginia	18	B	16	B	6	A	19	B	22	C
West Virginia	49	F	49	F	47	F	48	F	48	F
Mountain West										
Arizona	21	C	20	B	20	B	13	B	18	B
Colorado	5	A	5	A	5	A	4	A	2	A
Idaho	33	C	28	C	38	D	26	C	27	C
Montana	31	C	38	D	36	D	26	C	14	B
Nevada	25	C	16	B	32	C	26	C	32	C
New Mexico	30	C	36	D	39	D	35	C	35	C
Utah	8	A	3	A	3	A	2	A	4	A
Wyoming	28	C	22	C	35	C	23	C	37	D
Pacific										
Alaska	18	B	30	C	29	C	33	C	25	C
California	12	B	7	A	8	A	9	A	20	B
Hawaii	13	B	14	B	16	B	12	B	13	B
Oregon	9	A	13	B	14	B	16	B	10	A
Washington	4	A	2	A	2	A	3	A	3	A

1994 State Report Cards

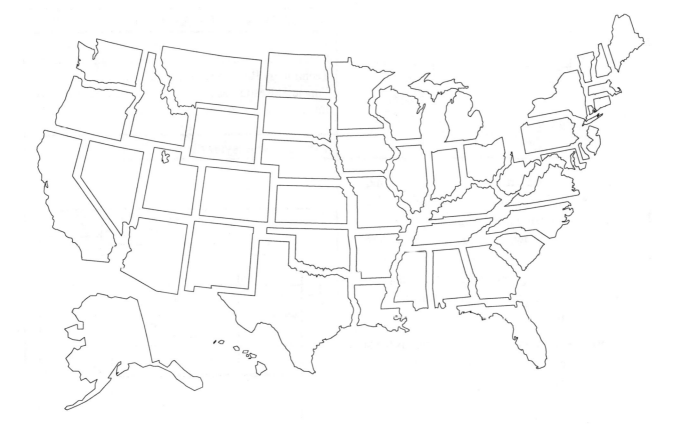

ALABAMA 1994 REPORT CARD

ECONOMIC PERFORMANCE	C
Employment	C
Earnings & Job Quality	C
Equity	C

BUSINESS VITALITY	A
Business Competitiveness	A
Entrepreneurial Energy	C
Structural Diversity	B

DEVELOPMENT CAPACITY	D
Human Resources	F
Technology Resources	C
Financial Resources	B
Infrastructure & Amenity Resources	D

Tax & Fiscal System	√

- **Economic Performance:** Alabama's economic performance was average across the board, but several promising trends emerge – long-term employment growth is at the median; a sharp increase in relative employer health coverage means improving job quality ratings; and change in income distribution is ninth best in the nation.

- **Business Vitality:** Alabama's grade is the sixth best in the nation. The state's businesses show strong structural diversity and are the most competitive in the South, led by the nation's second highest rate of new manufacturing capital investment.

- **Development Capacity:** Poor development resources continue to be a drag on Alabama's economy. Although the state has relatively strong financial resources, led by the nation's tenth highest ratio of loans to equity, infrastructure resources are weak and the state's human resources earn a failing mark.

Five Year Grade Trends

(Graph showing grades A–F for years 1990, 1991, 1992, 1993, 1994)

Key

Economic Performance	——
Business Vitality	≈≈≈≈
Development Capacity	- - -

For more information on how grades and ranks are calculated, see the Methodology section.
For a detailed explanation of indexes, refer to the individual index section.

WHERE ALABAMA RANKS – MEASURE BY MEASURE

50th 40th 30th 20th 10th 1st

ECONOMIC PERFORMANCE INDEX MEASURES

Employment
- Long-Term Employment Growth (25)
- Short-Term Employment Growth (28)
- Unemployment Rate (41)
- Unemployment Duration (14)

Earnings & Job Quality
- Average Annual Pay (31)
- Average Annual Pay Growth (29)
- Health Coverage (25)

Equity
- Poverty Rate (40)
- Income Distribution (41)
- Income Distribution Change (9)
- Rural/Urban Disparity (7)

Environmental, Social & Health Conditions
- Air Quality (15)
- Superfund Dumpsites (13)
- Hazardous Waste Generation (25)
- Surface Water Discharge (28)
- Infant Mortality (44)
- Crime Rate (28)
- Teen Pregnancy (39)
- Heart Disease (38)
- Cancer Cases (39)
- Infectious Diseases (13)

BUSINESS VITALITY INDEX MEASURES

Competitiveness of Existing Business
- Traded Sector Strength (23)
- Change in Traded Sector Strength (26)
- Business Closings (19)
- Manufacturing Capital Investment (2)

Entrepreneurial Energy
- New Companies (38)
- Change in New Companies (29)
- New Business Job Growth (12)

Structural Diversity
- Sectoral Diversity (5)
- Dynamic Diversity (31)

DEVELOPMENT CAPACITY INDEX MEASURES

Human Resources
- High School Graduation (44)
- High School Education Attainment (42)
- College Education Attainment (47)

Technology Resources
- Ph.D. Scientists & Engineers in Workforce (39)
- Science/Engineering Graduate Students (28)
- Patents Issued (46)
- University Research & Development (31)
- Federal Research & Development (7)
- SBIR Grants (12)

Financial Resources
- Commercial Bank Deposits (24)
- Loans to Deposits (21)
- Loans to Equity (10)
- Commercial & Industrial Loans (12)
- Comm. & Ind. Loans to Total Loans (20)
- Venture Capital Investments (18)
- SBIC Financings (38)

Infrastructure & Amenity Resources
- Highway Deficiency (36)
- Bridge Deficiency (34)
- Urban Mass Transit Availability (36)
- Energy Cost (15)
- Sewage Treatment Needs (13)
- Urban Housing Costs (5)
- Health Professional Shortage Areas (42)
- Tourism Spending (42)

TAX & FISCAL SYSTEM INDEX MEASURES

- Total Tax & Fiscal System Score (33)
- Fiscal Stability & Balanced Revenue (12)
- Tax Fairness (48)
- Fiscal Equalization (16)

50th 40th 30th 20th 10th 1st

ALASKA 1994 REPORT CARD

ECONOMIC PERFORMANCE	A
Employment	B
Earnings & Job Quality	C
Equity	A

BUSINESS VITALITY	C
Business Competitiveness	C
Entrepreneurial Energy	A
Structural Diversity	F

DEVELOPMENT CAPACITY	C
Human Resources	B
Technology Resources	C
Financial Resources	D
Infrastructure & Amenity Resources	B

Tax & Fiscal System	√

- **Economic Performance:** Alaska's economic performance was among the best in the nation. With very low poverty and good income distribution, Alaska's economy is among the best at spreading the benefits of growth. Employment growth and average pay are also top notch in Alaska, but high unemployment and the nation's second worst pay growth are cause for concern.

- **Business Vitality:** Alaska's average grade reflects a high level of entrepreneurial energy, led by strong new business job growth and the nation's second highest rate of new company formations, combined with very poor structural diversity.

- **Development Capacity:** Although Alaska's financial resources are poor, particularly judging by the ratio of loans to equity, the state has above average infrastructure and human resources. In fact, Alaska's high school education attainment is the nation's best.

Five Year Grade Trends

1990 1991 1992 1993 1994

Key	
Economic Performance	———
Business Vitality	≈≈≈
Development Capacity	- - -

For more information on how grades and ranks are calculated, see the Methodology section.
For a detailed explanation of indexes, refer to the individual index section.

WHERE ALASKA RANKS – MEASURE BY MEASURE

		50th	40th	30th	20th	10th	1st

ECONOMIC PERFORMANCE INDEX MEASURES

Employment
- Long-Term Employment Growth (8)
- Short-Term Employment Growth (4)
- Unemployment Rate (45)
- Unemployment Duration (10)

Earnings & Job Quality
- Average Annual Pay (4)
- Average Annual Pay Growth (49)
- Health Coverage (36)

Equity
- Poverty Rate (6)
- Income Distribution (21)
- Income Distribution Change (4)
- Rural/Urban Disparity (32)

Environmental, Social & Health Conditions
- Air Quality (28)
- Superfund Dumpsites (46)
- Hazardous Waste Generation (50)
- Surface Water Discharge (4)
- Infant Mortality (19)
- Crime Rate (31)
- Teen Pregnancy (45)
- Heart Disease (13)
- Cancer Cases (1)
- Infectious Diseases (47)

BUSINESS VITALITY INDEX MEASURES

Competitiveness of Existing Business
- Traded Sector Strength (4)
- Change in Traded Sector Strength (7)
- Business Closings (47)
- Manufacturing Capital Investment (40)

Entrepreneurial Energy
- New Companies (2)
- Change in New Companies (9)
- New Business Job Growth (9)

Structural Diversity
- Sectoral Diversity (43)
- Dynamic Diversity (50)

DEVELOPMENT CAPACITY INDEX MEASURES

Human Resources
- High School Graduation (32)
- High School Education Attainment (1)
- College Education Attainment (19)

Technology Resources
- Ph.D. Scientists & Engineers in Workforce (22)
- Science/Engineering Graduate Students (46)
- Patents Issued (43)
- University Research & Development (5)
- Federal Research & Development (15)
- SBIR Grants (25)

Financial Resources
- Commercial Bank Deposits (46)
- Loans to Deposits (32)
- Loans to Equity (50)
- Commercial & Industrial Loans (24)
- Comm. & Ind. Loans to Total Loans (4)
- Venture Capital Investments (37)
- SBIC Financings (44)

Infrastructure & Amenity Resources
- Highway Deficiency (12)
- Bridge Deficiency (7)
- Urban Mass Transit Availability (27)
- Energy Cost (42)
- Sewage Treatment Needs (33)
- Urban Housing Costs (14)
- Health Professional Shortage Areas (40)
- Tourism Spending (3)

TAX & FISCAL SYSTEM INDEX MEASURES
- Total Tax & Fiscal System Score (28)
- Fiscal Stability & Balanced Revenue (47)
- Tax Fairness (19)
- Fiscal Equalization (2)

		50th	40th	30th	20th	10th	1st

ARIZONA 1994 REPORT CARD

ECONOMIC PERFORMANCE	C
Employment	A
Earnings & Job Quality	D
Equity	C

BUSINESS VITALITY	F
Business Competitiveness	F
Entrepreneurial Energy	D
Structural Diversity	D

DEVELOPMENT CAPACITY	B
Human Resources	B
Technology Resources	B
Financial Resources	D
Infrastructure & Amenity Resources	B

Tax & Fiscal System	+

- **Economic Performance:** With increased job opportunities and distribution of income, Arizona improved one grade. The state has one of the nation's top ten job markets, led by improved rankings for short-term job growth and unemployment, but as with most states in the region, earnings and job quality are poor.

- **Business Vitality:** Arizona's business vitality is the worst in the nation. With a very weak traded sector, competitiveness earns a failing mark. The state's businesses are also poorly diversified.

- **Development Capacity:** Arizona's above average grade reflects strong development resources in every area except financial resources. Particular strengths include the best bridges in the country and strong high school and college attainment. Weaknesses include a worsening in the rank for scientists and engineers in the workforce and a low level of commercial lending activity.

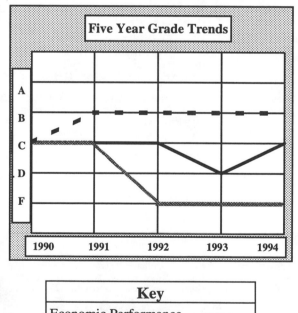

Five Year Grade Trends

Key	
Economic Performance	——
Business Vitality	≈≈≈≈
Development Capacity	- - -

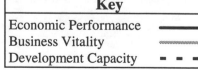

For more information on how grades and ranks are calculated, see the Methodology section.
For a detailed explanation of indexes, refer to the individual index section.

WHERE ARIZONA RANKS – MEASURE BY MEASURE

		50th	40th	30th	20th	10th	1st

ECONOMIC PERFORMANCE INDEX MEASURES

Employment
- Long-Term Employment Growth (4)
- Short-Term Employment Growth (14)
- Unemployment Rate (22)
- Unemployment Duration (22)

Earnings & Job Quality
- Average Annual Pay (26)
- Average Annual Pay Growth (41)
- Health Coverage (35)

Equity
- Poverty Rate (32)
- Income Distribution (32)
- Income Distribution Change (21)
- Rural/Urban Disparity (30)

Environmental, Social & Health Conditions
- Air Quality (38)
- Superfund Dumpsites (5)
- Hazardous Waste Generation (15)
- Surface Water Discharge (45)
- Infant Mortality (20)
- Crime Rate (48)
- Teen Pregnancy (49)
- Heart Disease (11)
- Cancer Cases (17)
- Infectious Diseases (49)

BUSINESS VITALITY INDEX MEASURES

Competitiveness of Existing Business
- Traded Sector Strength (47)
- Change in Traded Sector Strength (31)
- Business Closings (43)
- Manufacturing Capital Investment (23)

Entrepreneurial Energy
- New Companies (27)
- Change in New Companies (31)
- New Business Job Growth (35)

Structural Diversity
- Sectoral Diversity (23)
- Dynamic Diversity (47)

DEVELOPMENT CAPACITY INDEX MEASURES

Human Resources
- High School Graduation (31)
- High School Education Attainment (15)
- College Education Attainment (11)

Technology Resources
- Ph.D. Scientists & Engineers in Workforce (34)
- Science/Engineering Graduate Students (9)
- Patents Issued (18)
- University Research & Development (18)
- Federal Research & Development (22)
- SBIR Grants (20)

Financial Resources
- Commercial Bank Deposits (39)
- Loans to Deposits (35)
- Loans to Equity (36)
- Commercial & Industrial Loans (48)
- Comm. & Ind. Loans to Total Loans (47)
- Venture Capital Investments (23)
- SBIC Financings (9)

Infrastructure & Amenity Resources
- Highway Deficiency (18)
- Bridge Deficiency (1)
- Urban Mass Transit Availability (20)
- Energy Cost (38)
- Sewage Treatment Needs (32)
- Urban Housing Costs (35)
- Health Professional Shortage Areas (16)
- Tourism Spending (13)

TAX & FISCAL SYSTEM INDEX MEASURES

- Total Tax & Fiscal System Score (7)
- Fiscal Stability & Balanced Revenue (7)
- Tax Fairness (5)
- Fiscal Equalization (39)

		50th	40th	30th	20th	10th	1st

The 1994 Development Report Card
41

ARKANSAS 1994 REPORT CARD

ECONOMIC PERFORMANCE	C
Employment	B
Earnings & Job Quality	D
Equity	B

BUSINESS VITALITY	D
Business Competitiveness	C
Entrepreneurial Energy	C
Structural Diversity	D

DEVELOPMENT CAPACITY	F
Human Resources	D
Technology Resources	F
Financial Resources	F
Infrastructure & Amenity Resources	C

Tax & Fiscal System	√

- **Economic Performance:** Arkansas benefits from above average job opportunities, but with very poor pay and employer health coverage, job quality is poor. Although poverty remains high, a top ten rank in the change in income distribution results in the second best score in the South on measures of equity.

- **Business Vitality:** Arkansas' business vitality grade dropped steeply from last year's A. While the state still ranks well in new company formation, an increase in business closings reflects weakened competitiveness.

- **Development Capacity:** Arkansas' development resources continue to be among the weakest in the U.S. – highlighted by very poor college attainment and financial resources, as well as the worst technology resources in the U.S. On the bright side are an above median high school graduation rate and good infrastructure resources, particularly highways and sewage treatment facilities.

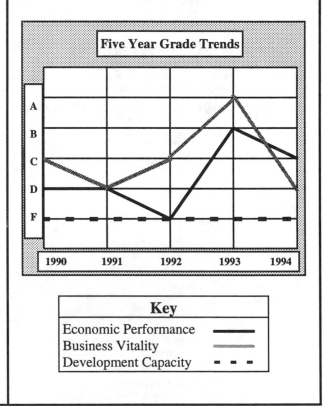

For more information on how grades and ranks are calculated, see the Methodology section.
For a detailed explanation of indexes, refer to the individual index section.

WHERE ARKANSAS RANKS – MEASURE BY MEASURE

50th 40th 30th 20th 10th 1st

ECONOMIC PERFORMANCE INDEX MEASURES

Employment
- Long-Term Employment Growth (21)
- Short-Term Employment Growth (25)
- Unemployment Rate (22)
- Unemployment Duration (13)

Earnings & Job Quality
- Average Annual Pay (46)
- Average Annual Pay Growth (9)
- Health Coverage (45)

Equity
- Poverty Rate (41)
- Income Distribution (34)
- Income Distribution Change (8)
- Rural/Urban Disparity (6)

Environmental, Social & Health Conditions
- Air Quality (1)
- Superfund Dumpsites (25)
- Hazardous Waste Generation (33)
- Surface Water Discharge (34)
- Infant Mortality (30)
- Crime Rate (21)
- Teen Pregnancy (47)
- Heart Disease (31)
- Cancer Cases (47)
- Infectious Diseases (33)

BUSINESS VITALITY INDEX MEASURES

Competitiveness of Existing Business
- Traded Sector Strength (27)
- Change in Traded Sector Strength (21)
- Business Closings (35)
- Manufacturing Capital Investment (14)

Entrepreneurial Energy
- New Companies (19)
- Change in New Companies (24)
- New Business Job Growth (42)

Structural Diversity
- Sectoral Diversity (31)
- Dynamic Diversity (33)

DEVELOPMENT CAPACITY INDEX MEASURES

Human Resources
- High School Graduation (21)
- High School Education Attainment (42)
- College Education Attainment (49)

Technology Resources
- Ph.D. Scientists & Engineers in Workforce (50)
- Science/Engineering Graduate Students (50)
- Patents Issued (45)
- University Research & Development (49)
- Federal Research & Development (47)
- SBIR Grants (42)

Financial Resources
- Commercial Bank Deposits (16)
- Loans to Deposits (44)
- Loans to Equity (43)
- Commercial & Industrial Loans (42)
- Comm. & Ind. Loans to Total Loans (43)
- Venture Capital Investments (37)
- SBIC Financings (32)

Infrastructure & Amenity Resources
- Highway Deficiency (9)
- Bridge Deficiency (33)
- Urban Mass Transit Availability (45)
- Energy Cost (32)
- Sewage Treatment Needs (5)
- Urban Housing Costs (8)
- Health Professional Shortage Areas (39)
- Tourism Spending (32)

TAX & FISCAL SYSTEM INDEX MEASURES

- Total Tax & Fiscal System Score (21)
- Fiscal Stability & Balanced Revenue (16)
- Tax Fairness (41)
- Fiscal Equalization (5)

50th 40th 30th 20th 10th 1st

CALIFORNIA 1994 REPORT CARD

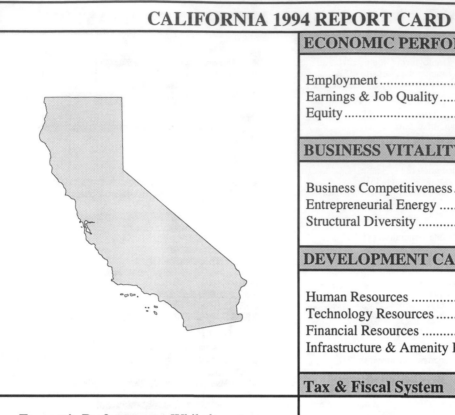

ECONOMIC PERFORMANCE	F
Employment	D
Earnings & Job Quality	C
Equity	F

BUSINESS VITALITY	C
Business Competitiveness	D
Entrepreneurial Energy	C
Structural Diversity	C

DEVELOPMENT CAPACITY	B
Human Resources	C
Technology Resources	A
Financial Resources	B
Infrastructure & Amenity Resources	D

Tax & Fiscal System	+

- **Economic Performance:** While long-term employment growth and average annual pay were high, short-term employment growth and unemployment are among the nation's worst. This does not bode well for equity, already worst in the country, with high poverty and poor income distribution.

- **Business Vitality:** The state has good and bad news: a strong traded sector and diverse economy, but many business closings coupled with weak growth in new companies and a bottom-ten dynamic diversity ranking as employment in many key sectors declines.

- **Development Capacity:** There is hope in California's good human and technology resources and venture capital (though future Federal R&D may fall, and high school graduation is low). Physical infrastructure is inferior in urban housing, energy costs, and highways.

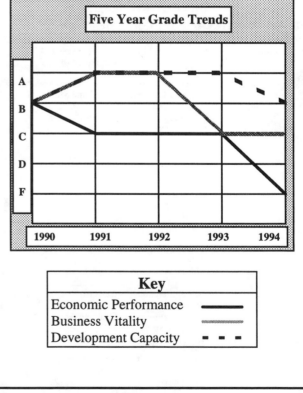

Five Year Grade Trends

Key
Economic Performance ———
Business Vitality ———
Development Capacity - - -

For more information on how grades and ranks are calculated, see the Methodology section.
For a detailed explanation of indexes, refer to the individual index section.

WHERE CALIFORNIA RANKS – MEASURE BY MEASURE

ECONOMIC PERFORMANCE INDEX MEASURES

Employment	Long-Term Employment Growth (17)
	Short-Term Employment Growth (46)
	Unemployment Rate (49)
	Unemployment Duration (34)
Earnings &	Average Annual Pay (6)
Job Quality	Average Annual Pay Growth (23)
	Health Coverage (43)
Equity	Poverty Rate (38)
	Income Distribution (46)
	Income Distribution Change (45)
	Rural/Urban Disparity (50)
Environmental,	Air Quality (50)
Social &	Superfund Dumpsites (8)
Health	Hazardous Waste Generation (35)
Conditions	Surface Water Discharge (5)
	Infant Mortality (6)
	Crime Rate (47)
	Teen Pregnancy (40)
	Heart Disease (23)
	Cancer Cases (8)
	Infectious Diseases (45)

BUSINESS VITALITY INDEX MEASURES

Competitiveness	Traded Sector Strength (14)
of Existing	Change in Traded Sector Strength (32)
Business	Business Closings (45)
	Manufacturing Capital Investment (36)
Entrepreneurial	New Companies (4)
Energy	Change in New Companies (45)
	New Business Job Growth (28)
Structural	Sectoral Diversity (8)
Diversity	Dynamic Diversity (42)

DEVELOPMENT CAPACITY INDEX MEASURES

Human	High School Graduation (42)
Resources	High School Education Attainment (19)
	College Education Attainment (7)
Technology	Ph.D. Scientists & Engineers in Workforce (11)
Resources	Science/Engineering Graduate Students (30)
	Patents Issued (8)
	University Research & Development (21)
	Federal Research & Development (5)
	SBIR Grants (7)
Financial	Commercial Bank Deposits (36)
Resources	Loans to Deposits (24)
	Loans to Equity (28)
	Commercial & Industrial Loans (23)
	Comm. & Ind. Loans to Total Loans (29)
	Venture Capital Investments (2)
	SBIC Financings (11)
Infrastructure	Highway Deficiency (43)
& Amenity	Bridge Deficiency (18)
Resources	Urban Mass Transit Availability (7)
	Energy Cost (45)
	Sewage Treatment Needs (24)
	Urban Housing Costs (49)
	Health Professional Shortage Areas (19)
	Tourism Spending (16)

TAX & FISCAL SYSTEM INDEX MEASURES

	Total Tax & Fiscal System Score (3)
	Fiscal Stability & Balanced Revenue (5)
	Tax Fairness (1)
	Fiscal Equalization (30)

(Horizontal bar chart with scale markings: 50th, 40th, 30th, 20th, 10th, 1st)

COLORADO 1994 REPORT CARD

ECONOMIC PERFORMANCE   A

Employment .... A
Earnings & Job Quality C
Equity .... A

BUSINESS VITALITY   A

Business Competitiveness C
Entrepreneurial Energy .... B
Structural Diversity .... A

DEVELOPMENT CAPACITY   A

Human Resources .... A
Technology Resources .... A
Financial Resources C
Infrastructure & Amenity Resources .... A

Tax & Fiscal System   +

- **Economic Performance:** Colorado's economic performance grade has steadily improved one letter grade per year, from a D in 1991 to an A this year. With low unemployment and rapid short-term employment growth, job prospects are good. Also, while measures of job quality rate only average, the state has low poverty and scores well on measures of equity.

- **Business Vitality:** Led by the nation's second most structurally diverse economy, Colorado again earns the highest grade for vitality. The state also boasts strong entrepreneurial energy.

- **Development Capacity:** With the nation's best infrastructure and amenity resources, as well as human and technology resources that rank among the nation's top ten, Colorado's development resources are the second best in the nation. Financial resources, marked by low levels of lending activity, are the only weakness.

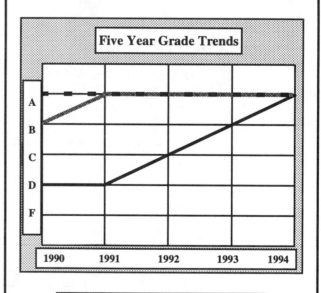

Five Year Grade Trends

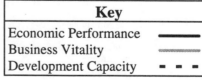

Key	
Economic Performance	——
Business Vitality	▨▨▨
Development Capacity	- - -

For more information on how grades and ranks are calculated, see the Methodology section.
For a detailed explanation of indexes, refer to the individual index section.

WHERE COLORADO RANKS – MEASURE BY MEASURE

Scale across top: 50th — 40th — 30th — 20th — 10th — 1st

ECONOMIC PERFORMANCE INDEX MEASURES

Employment
- Long-Term Employment Growth (29)
- Short-Term Employment Growth (3)
- Unemployment Rate (12)
- Unemployment Duration (15)

Earnings & Job Quality
- Average Annual Pay (16)
- Average Annual Pay Growth (40)
- Health Coverage (21)

Equity
- Poverty Rate (12)
- Income Distribution (22)
- Income Distribution Change (5)
- Rural/Urban Disparity (30)

Environmental, Social & Health Conditions
- Air Quality (32)
- Superfund Dumpsites (27)
- Hazardous Waste Generation (27)
- Surface Water Discharge (17)
- Infant Mortality (18)
- Crime Rate (39)
- Teen Pregnancy (25)
- Heart Disease (1)
- Cancer Cases (3)
- Infectious Diseases (26)

BUSINESS VITALITY INDEX MEASURES

Competitiveness of Existing Business
- Traded Sector Strength (28)
- Change in Traded Sector Strength (27)
- Business Closings (29)
- Manufacturing Capital Investment (24)

Entrepreneurial Energy
- New Companies (13)
- Change in New Companies (32)
- New Business Job Growth (20)

Structural Diversity
- Sectoral Diversity (6)
- Dynamic Diversity (4)

DEVELOPMENT CAPACITY INDEX MEASURES

Human Resources
- High School Graduation (26)
- High School Education Attainment (2)
- College Education Attainment (1)

Technology Resources
- Ph.D. Scientists & Engineers in Workforce (5)
- Science/Engineering Graduate Students (2)
- Patents Issued (11)
- University Research & Development (12)
- Federal Research & Development (3)
- SBIR Grants (9)

Financial Resources
- Commercial Bank Deposits (30)
- Loans to Deposits (48)
- Loans to Equity (33)
- Commercial & Industrial Loans (47)
- Comm. & Ind. Loans to Total Loans (42)
- Venture Capital Investments (5)
- SBIC Financings (12)

Infrastructure & Amenity Resources
- Highway Deficiency (14)
- Bridge Deficiency (12)
- Urban Mass Transit Availability (11)
- Energy Cost (21)
- Sewage Treatment Needs (11)
- Urban Housing Costs (13)
- Health Professional Shortage Areas (9)
- Tourism Spending (6)

TAX & FISCAL SYSTEM INDEX MEASURES
- Total Tax & Fiscal System Score (14)
- Fiscal Stability & Balanced Revenue (4)
- Tax Fairness (10)
- Fiscal Equalization (45)

Scale across bottom: 50th — 40th — 30th — 20th — 10th — 1st

CONNECTICUT 1994 REPORT CARD

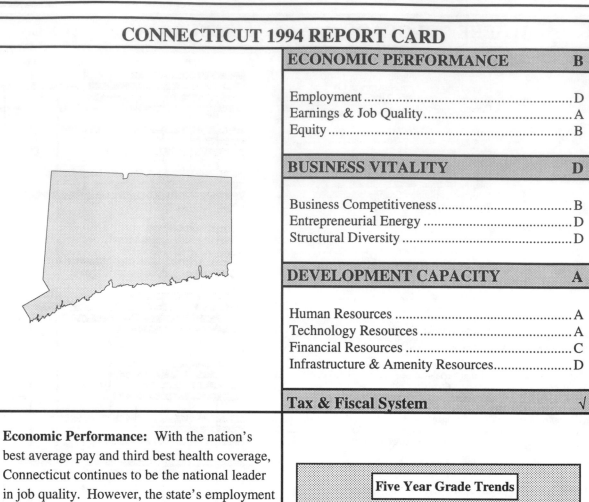

ECONOMIC PERFORMANCE	B
Employment	D
Earnings & Job Quality	A
Equity	B

BUSINESS VITALITY	D
Business Competitiveness	B
Entrepreneurial Energy	D
Structural Diversity	D

DEVELOPMENT CAPACITY	A
Human Resources	A
Technology Resources	A
Financial Resources	C
Infrastructure & Amenity Resources	D

Tax & Fiscal System	√

- **Economic Performance:** With the nation's best average pay and third best health coverage, Connecticut continues to be the national leader in job quality. However, the state's employment picture remains poor – long-term employment growth is very slow and unemployment duration is the longest in the nation.

- **Business Vitality:** Connecticut's vitality grade dropped for the third straight year. Though still claiming the nation's strongest traded sector, competitiveness was hurt by an increase in business failures. Low entrepreneurial energy and poor diversification remain weaknesses.

- **Development Capacity:** The state's development resources are very strong. With an improvement in its comparative high school graduation rate, Connecticut now has the nation's best human resources to go with its top notch technology resources. Infrastructure resources remain the major weakness.

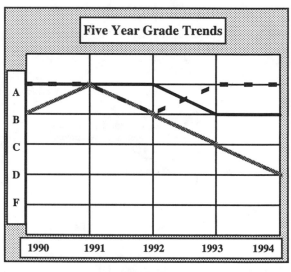

Five Year Grade Trends

A B C D F

1990 1991 1992 1993 1994

Key	
Economic Performance	———
Business Vitality	≈≈≈≈≈
Development Capacity	- - -

For more information on how grades and ranks are calculated, see the Methodology section.
For a detailed explanation of indexes, refer to the individual index section.

WHERE CONNECTICUT RANKS – MEASURE BY MEASURE

Scale (top): 50th | 40th | 30th | 20th | 10th | 1st

ECONOMIC PERFORMANCE INDEX MEASURES

Employment
- Long-Term Employment Growth (42)
- Short-Term Employment Growth (45)
- Unemployment Rate (22)
- Unemployment Duration (50)

Earnings & Job Quality
- Average Annual Pay (1)
- Average Annual Pay Growth (6)
- Health Coverage (3)

Equity
- Poverty Rate (4)
- Income Distribution (4)
- Income Distribution Change (40)
- Rural/Urban Disparity (37)

Environmental, Social & Health Conditions
- Air Quality (47)
- Superfund Dumpsites (24)
- Hazardous Waste Generation (37)
- Surface Water Discharge (41)
- Infant Mortality (N/A)
- Crime Rate (24)
- Teen Pregnancy (6)
- Heart Disease (19)
- Cancer Cases (35)
- Infectious Diseases (22)

BUSINESS VITALITY INDEX MEASURES

Competitiveness of Existing Business
- Traded Sector Strength (1)
- Change in Traded Sector Strength (9)
- Business Closings (34)
- Manufacturing Capital Investment (44)

Entrepreneurial Energy
- New Companies (33)
- Change in New Companies (17)
- New Business Job Growth (43)

Structural Diversity
- Sectoral Diversity (36)
- Dynamic Diversity (39)

DEVELOPMENT CAPACITY INDEX MEASURES

Human Resources
- High School Graduation (16)
- High School Education Attainment (5)
- College Education Attainment (3)

Technology Resources
- Ph.D. Scientists & Engineers in Workforce (14)
- Science/Engineering Graduate Students (31)
- Patents Issued (2)
- University Research & Development (6)
- Federal Research & Development (14)
- SBIR Grants (3)

Financial Resources
- Commercial Bank Deposits (42)
- Loans to Deposits (28)
- Loans to Equity (17)
- Commercial & Industrial Loans (30)
- Comm. & Ind. Loans to Total Loans (14)
- Venture Capital Investments (14)
- SBIC Financings (20)

Infrastructure & Amenity Resources
- Highway Deficiency (11)
- Bridge Deficiency (32)
- Urban Mass Transit Availability (22)
- Energy Cost (47)
- Sewage Treatment Needs (45)
- Urban Housing Costs (38)
- Health Professional Shortage Areas (5)
- Tourism Spending (49)

TAX & FISCAL SYSTEM INDEX MEASURES

- Total Tax & Fiscal System Score (23)
- Fiscal Stability & Balanced Revenue (19)
- Tax Fairness (12)
- Fiscal Equalization (42)

Scale (bottom): 50th | 40th | 30th | 20th | 10th | 1st

DELAWARE 1994 REPORT CARD

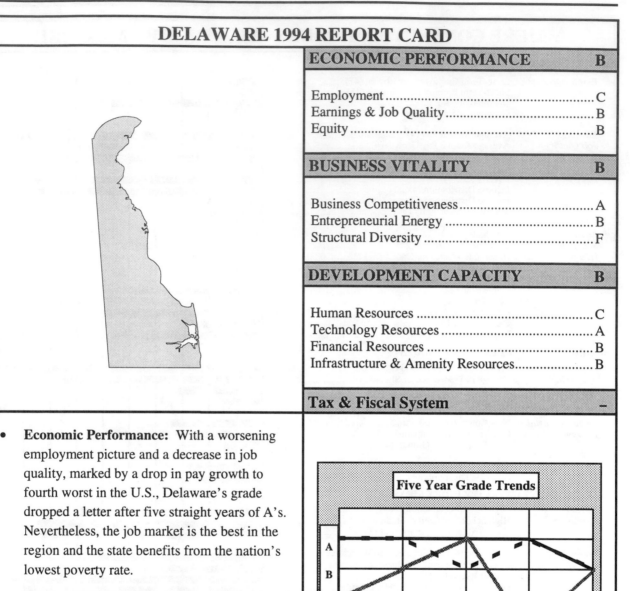

ECONOMIC PERFORMANCE	B
Employment	C
Earnings & Job Quality	B
Equity	B

BUSINESS VITALITY	B
Business Competitiveness	A
Entrepreneurial Energy	B
Structural Diversity	F

DEVELOPMENT CAPACITY	B
Human Resources	C
Technology Resources	A
Financial Resources	B
Infrastructure & Amenity Resources	B

Tax & Fiscal System	–

- **Economic Performance:** With a worsening employment picture and a decrease in job quality, marked by a drop in pay growth to fourth worst in the U.S., Delaware's grade dropped a letter after five straight years of A's. Nevertheless, the job market is the best in the region and the state benefits from the nation's lowest poverty rate.

- **Business Vitality:** Delaware's grade improved two letters with a resurgence in entrepreneurial energy, including the nation's best new business job growth. The state's businesses continue to be very competitive, but lack diversity.

- **Development Capacity:** Delaware's development resources are strong, particularly the state's technology resources, which benefit from the nation's highest ranking for scientists and engineers. With the region's second worst high school graduation rate, however, human resources are only average.

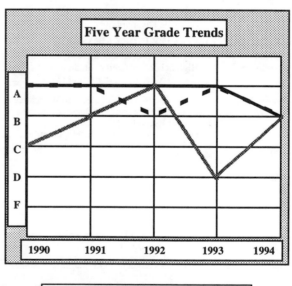

Five Year Grade Trends

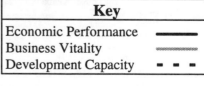

Key	
Economic Performance	————
Business Vitality	≈≈≈≈
Development Capacity	- - -

For more information on how grades and ranks are calculated, see the Methodology section.
For a detailed explanation of indexes, refer to the individual index section.

WHERE DELAWARE RANKS – MEASURE BY MEASURE

ECONOMIC PERFORMANCE INDEX MEASURES

		50th	40th	30th	20th	10th	1st

Employment
- Long-Term Employment Growth (13)
- Short-Term Employment Growth (22)
- Unemployment Rate (13)
- Unemployment Duration (38)

Earnings & Job Quality
- Average Annual Pay (10)
- Average Annual Pay Growth (47)
- Health Coverage (5)

Equity
- Poverty Rate (1)
- Income Distribution (6)
- Income Distribution Change (30)
- Rural/Urban Disparity (49)

Environmental, Social & Health Conditions
- Air Quality (42)
- Superfund Dumpsites (50)
- Hazardous Waste Generation (11)
- Surface Water Discharge (49)
- Infant Mortality (23)
- Crime Rate (22)
- Teen Pregnancy (30)
- Heart Disease (34)
- Cancer Cases (42)
- Infectious Diseases (34)

BUSINESS VITALITY INDEX MEASURES

Competitiveness of Existing Business
- Traded Sector Strength (3)
- Change in Traded Sector Strength (17)
- Business Closings (1)
- Manufacturing Capital Investment (27)

Entrepreneurial Energy
- New Companies (20)
- Change in New Companies (39)
- New Business Job Growth (1)

Structural Diversity
- Sectoral Diversity (49)
- Dynamic Diversity (43)

DEVELOPMENT CAPACITY INDEX MEASURES

Human Resources
- High School Graduation (40)
- High School Education Attainment (24)
- College Education Attainment (25)

Technology Resources
- Ph.D. Scientists & Engineers in Workforce (1)
- Science/Engineering Graduate Students (4)
- Patents Issued (1)
- University Research & Development (23)
- Federal Research & Development (40)
- SBIR Grants (22)

Financial Resources
- Commercial Bank Deposits (1)
- Loans to Deposits (1)
- Loans to Equity (26)
- Commercial & Industrial Loans (4)
- Comm. & Ind. Loans to Total Loans (50)
- Venture Capital Investments (7)
- SBIC Financings (40)

Infrastructure & Amenity Resources
- Highway Deficiency (23)
- Bridge Deficiency (11)
- Urban Mass Transit Availability (24)
- Energy Cost (30)
- Sewage Treatment Needs (25)
- Urban Housing Costs (33)
- Health Professional Shortage Areas (4)
- Tourism Spending (30)

TAX & FISCAL SYSTEM INDEX MEASURES

- Total Tax & Fiscal System Score (39)
- Fiscal Stability & Balanced Revenue (42)
- Tax Fairness (24)
- Fiscal Equalization (25)

		50th	40th	30th	20th	10th	1st

FLORIDA 1994 REPORT CARD

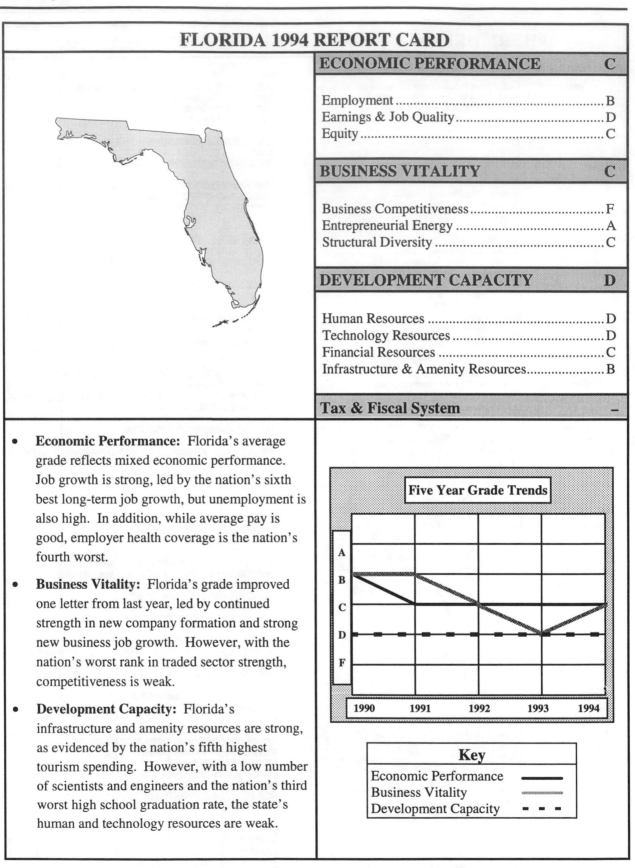

ECONOMIC PERFORMANCE	C
Employment	B
Earnings & Job Quality	D
Equity	C

BUSINESS VITALITY	C
Business Competitiveness	F
Entrepreneurial Energy	A
Structural Diversity	C

DEVELOPMENT CAPACITY	D
Human Resources	D
Technology Resources	D
Financial Resources	C
Infrastructure & Amenity Resources	B

Tax & Fiscal System	–

- **Economic Performance:** Florida's average grade reflects mixed economic performance. Job growth is strong, led by the nation's sixth best long-term job growth, but unemployment is also high. In addition, while average pay is good, employer health coverage is the nation's fourth worst.

- **Business Vitality:** Florida's grade improved one letter from last year, led by continued strength in new company formation and strong new business job growth. However, with the nation's worst rank in traded sector strength, competitiveness is weak.

- **Development Capacity:** Florida's infrastructure and amenity resources are strong, as evidenced by the nation's fifth highest tourism spending. However, with a low number of scientists and engineers and the nation's third worst high school graduation rate, the state's human and technology resources are weak.

Five Year Grade Trends

Key	
Economic Performance	——
Business Vitality	≈≈≈
Development Capacity	- - -

For more information on how grades and ranks are calculated, see the Methodology section.
For a detailed explanation of indexes, refer to the individual index section.

WHERE FLORIDA RANKS – MEASURE BY MEASURE

ECONOMIC PERFORMANCE INDEX MEASURES

Employment	Long-Term Employment Growth (6)
	Short-Term Employment Growth (13)
	Unemployment Rate (32)
	Unemployment Duration (33)
Earnings & Job Quality	Average Annual Pay (27)
	Average Annual Pay Growth (23)
	Health Coverage (47)
Equity	Poverty Rate (33)
	Income Distribution (33)
	Income Distribution Change (21)
	Rural/Urban Disparity (12)
Environmental, Social & Health Conditions	Air Quality (26)
	Superfund Dumpsites (21)
	Hazardous Waste Generation (13)
	Surface Water Discharge (7)
	Infant Mortality (27)
	Crime Rate (50)
	Teen Pregnancy (34)
	Heart Disease (15)
	Cancer Cases (50)
	Infectious Diseases (41)

BUSINESS VITALITY INDEX MEASURES

Competitiveness of Existing Business	Traded Sector Strength (50)
	Change in Traded Sector Strength (48)
	Business Closings (44)
	Manufacturing Capital Investment (33)
Entrepreneurial Energy	New Companies (6)
	Change in New Companies (22)
	New Business Job Growth (11)
Structural Diversity	Sectoral Diversity (12)
	Dynamic Diversity (40)

DEVELOPMENT CAPACITY INDEX MEASURES

Human Resources	High School Graduation (48)
	High School Education Attainment (24)
	College Education Attainment (25)
Technology Resources	Ph.D. Scientists & Engineers in Workforce (49)
	Science/Engineering Graduate Students (41)
	Patents Issued (28)
	University Research & Development (45)
	Federal Research & Development (19)
	SBIR Grants (26)
Financial Resources	Commercial Bank Deposits (22)
	Loans to Deposits (29)
	Loans to Equity (9)
	Commercial & Industrial Loans (41)
	Comm. & Ind. Loans to Total Loans (46)
	Venture Capital Investments (20)
	SBIC Financings (8)
Infrastructure & Amenity Resources	Highway Deficiency (25)
	Bridge Deficiency (9)
	Urban Mass Transit Availability (17)
	Energy Cost (34)
	Sewage Treatment Needs (39)
	Urban Housing Costs (39)
	Health Professional Shortage Areas (15)
	Tourism Spending (5)

TAX & FISCAL SYSTEM INDEX MEASURES

	Total Tax & Fiscal System Score (43)
	Fiscal Stability & Balanced Revenue (36)
	Tax Fairness (42)
	Fiscal Equalization (29)

Chart scale: 50th, 40th, 30th, 20th, 10th, 1st

GEORGIA 1994 REPORT CARD

ECONOMIC PERFORMANCE	C
Employment	B
Earnings & Job Quality	C
Equity	D

BUSINESS VITALITY	B
Business Competitiveness	C
Entrepreneurial Energy	C
Structural Diversity	B

DEVELOPMENT CAPACITY	C
Human Resources	D
Technology Resources	D
Financial Resources	A
Infrastructure & Amenity Resources	A

Tax & Fiscal System	√

- **Economic Performance:** With the nation's fifth best short-term employment growth figures and the second best job opportunity in the South, Georgia's grade improved from last year. However, earnings and job quality are only average, and with the fourth worst income distribution in the U.S., the benefits of growth are spread inequitably.

- **Business Vitality:** Georgia's business vitality is strong, led by a relatively diverse economy. The state also scores in the top 20 on traded sector strength, new companies, and manufacturing capital investments.

- **Development Capacity:** One of only two Southern states with a grade better than D, Georgia boasts top notch financial and infrastructure resources, led by the nation's best highways. However, technology resources are weak, and with the nation's fifth worst high school graduation rate, so are Georgia's human resources.

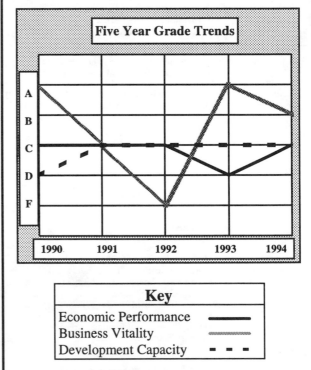

Five Year Grade Trends

Key
Economic Performance ———
Business Vitality ————
Development Capacity – – –

For more information on how grades and ranks are calculated, see the Methodology section.
For a detailed explanation of indexes, refer to the individual index section.

WHERE GEORGIA RANKS – MEASURE BY MEASURE

| | | 50th | 40th | 30th | 20th | 10th | 1st |

ECONOMIC PERFORMANCE INDEX MEASURES

Employment
- Long-Term Employment Growth (9)
- Short-Term Employment Growth (5)
- Unemployment Rate (18)
- Unemployment Duration (38)

Earnings & Job Quality
- Average Annual Pay (21)
- Average Annual Pay Growth (23)
- Health Coverage (39)

Equity
- Poverty Rate (42)
- Income Distribution (47)
- Income Distribution Change (42)
- Rural/Urban Disparity (2)

Environmental, Social & Health Conditions
- Air Quality (32)
- Superfund Dumpsites (4)
- Hazardous Waste Generation (22)
- Surface Water Discharge (20)
- Infant Mortality (41)
- Crime Rate (44)
- Teen Pregnancy (43)
- Heart Disease (36)
- Cancer Cases (10)
- Infectious Diseases (35)

BUSINESS VITALITY INDEX MEASURES

Competitiveness of Existing Business
- Traded Sector Strength (17)
- Change in Traded Sector Strength (12)
- Business Closings (46)
- Manufacturing Capital Investment (19)

Entrepreneurial Energy
- New Companies (18)
- Change in New Companies (14)
- New Business Job Growth (44)

Structural Diversity
- Sectoral Diversity (13)
- Dynamic Diversity (22)

DEVELOPMENT CAPACITY INDEX MEASURES

Human Resources
- High School Graduation (46)
- High School Education Attainment (40)
- College Education Attainment (19)

Technology Resources
- Ph.D. Scientists & Engineers in Workforce (45)
- Science/Engineering Graduate Students (37)
- Patents Issued (37)
- University Research & Development (20)
- Federal Research & Development (35)
- SBIR Grants (32)

Financial Resources
- Commercial Bank Deposits (21)
- Loans to Deposits (9)
- Loans to Equity (23)
- Commercial & Industrial Loans (10)
- Comm. & Ind. Loans to Total Loans (10)
- Venture Capital Investments (9)
- SBIC Financings (30)

Infrastructure & Amenity Resources
- Highway Deficiency (1)
- Bridge Deficiency (21)
- Urban Mass Transit Availability (8)
- Energy Cost (29)
- Sewage Treatment Needs (28)
- Urban Housing Costs (25)
- Health Professional Shortage Areas (38)
- Tourism Spending (8)

TAX & FISCAL SYSTEM INDEX MEASURES

- Total Tax & Fiscal System Score (30)
- Fiscal Stability & Balanced Revenue (17)
- Tax Fairness (40)
- Fiscal Equalization (18)

| | | 50th | 40th | 30th | 20th | 10th | 1st |

HAWAII 1994 REPORT CARD

ECONOMIC PERFORMANCE	A
Employment	A
Earnings & Job Quality	A
Equity	A

BUSINESS VITALITY	F
Business Competitiveness	D
Entrepreneurial Energy	C
Structural Diversity	F

DEVELOPMENT CAPACITY	B
Human Resources	A
Technology Resources	C
Financial Resources	B
Infrastructure & Amenity Resources	C

Tax & Fiscal System	+

- **Economic Performance:** Hawaii had the best performing economy as long-term employment growth and the unemployment rate were the fifth best in the country. Unemployment duration was the shortest. Job quality is excellent, health coverage is second best, and already strong earnings are getting better. And to top it off, equity is ninth best.

- **Business Vitality:** While Hawaii's tourism economy provides some economic benefits, it leaves the state vulnerable. It ranks 47th in diversity and has poor traded sector strength (tourism is low wage) and manufacturing capital investment is low.

- **Development Capacity:** Hawaii's overall resources are strong though there are weaknesses in infrastructure with high energy and urban housing costs. A high number of the population has a high school education (5th in graduation, 7th in attainment) and the state has good financial resources and loan activity.

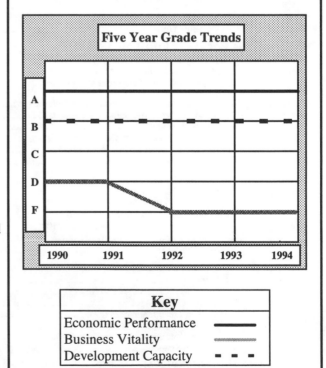

Five Year Grade Trends

Key	
Economic Performance	——
Business Vitality	▨▨▨
Development Capacity	- - -

For more information on how grades and ranks are calculated, see the Methodology section.
For a detailed explanation of indexes, refer to the individual index section.

WHERE HAWAII RANKS – MEASURE BY MEASURE

50th 40th 30th 20th 10th 1st

ECONOMIC PERFORMANCE INDEX MEASURES

Employment
Long-Term Employment Growth (5)
Short-Term Employment Growth (33)
Unemployment Rate (5)
Unemployment Duration (1)

Earnings & Job Quality
Average Annual Pay (12)
Average Annual Pay Growth (5)
Health Coverage (2)

Equity
Poverty Rate (14)
Income Distribution (14)
Income Distribution Change (10)
Rural/Urban Disparity (32)

Environmental, Social & Health Conditions
Air Quality (1)
Superfund Dumpsites (16)
Hazardous Waste Generation (2)
Surface Water Discharge (1)
Infant Mortality (10)
Crime Rate (40)
Teen Pregnancy (27)
Heart Disease (3)
Cancer Cases (4)
Infectious Diseases (37)

BUSINESS VITALITY INDEX MEASURES

Competitiveness of Existing Business
Traded Sector Strength (46)
Change in Traded Sector Strength (22)
Business Closings (18)
Manufacturing Capital Investment (49)

Entrepreneurial Energy
New Companies (31)
Change in New Companies (30)
New Business Job Growth (10)

Structural Diversity
Sectoral Diversity (44)
Dynamic Diversity (49)

DEVELOPMENT CAPACITY INDEX MEASURES

Human Resources
High School Graduation (23)
High School Education Attainment (5)
College Education Attainment (7)

Technology Resources
Ph.D. Scientists & Engineers in Workforce (19)
Science/Engineering Graduate Students (15)
Patents Issued (48)
University Research & Development (25)
Federal Research & Development (28)
SBIR Grants (10)

Financial Resources
Commercial Bank Deposits (8)
Loans to Deposits (4)
Loans to Equity (20)
Commercial & Industrial Loans (8)
Comm. & Ind. Loans to Total Loans (15)
Venture Capital Investments (37)
SBIC Financings (44)

Infrastructure & Amenity Resources
Highway Deficiency (35)
Bridge Deficiency (48)
Urban Mass Transit Availability (6)
Energy Cost (43)
Sewage Treatment Needs (16)
Urban Housing Costs (50)
Health Professional Shortage Areas (1)
Tourism Spending (2)

TAX & FISCAL SYSTEM INDEX MEASURES

Total Tax & Fiscal System Score (5)
Fiscal Stability & Balanced Revenue (27)
Tax Fairness (14)
Fiscal Equalization (9)

50th 40th 30th 20th 10th 1st

IDAHO 1994 REPORT CARD

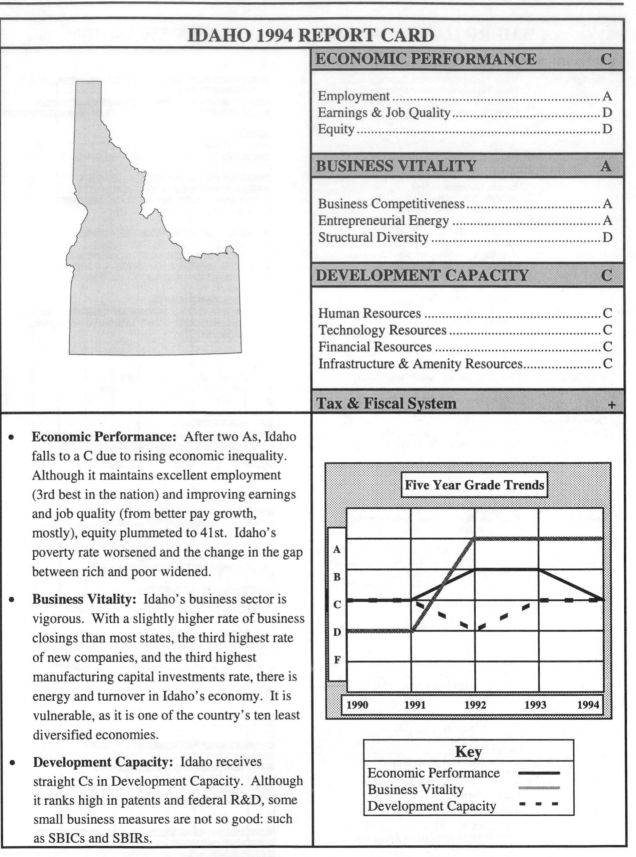

ECONOMIC PERFORMANCE	C
Employment	A
Earnings & Job Quality	D
Equity	D

BUSINESS VITALITY	A
Business Competitiveness	A
Entrepreneurial Energy	A
Structural Diversity	D

DEVELOPMENT CAPACITY	C
Human Resources	C
Technology Resources	C
Financial Resources	C
Infrastructure & Amenity Resources	C

Tax & Fiscal System	+

- **Economic Performance:** After two As, Idaho falls to a C due to rising economic inequality. Although it maintains excellent employment (3rd best in the nation) and improving earnings and job quality (from better pay growth, mostly), equity plummeted to 41st. Idaho's poverty rate worsened and the change in the gap between rich and poor widened.

- **Business Vitality:** Idaho's business sector is vigorous. With a slightly higher rate of business closings than most states, the third highest rate of new companies, and the third highest manufacturing capital investments rate, there is energy and turnover in Idaho's economy. It is vulnerable, as it is one of the country's ten least diversified economies.

- **Development Capacity:** Idaho receives straight Cs in Development Capacity. Although it ranks high in patents and federal R&D, some small business measures are not so good: such as SBICs and SBIRs.

Five Year Grade Trends

| | 1990 | 1991 | 1992 | 1993 | 1994 |

A B C D F

Key

Economic Performance ——————
Business Vitality ▒▒▒▒▒▒▒
Development Capacity - - - -

For more information on how grades and ranks are calculated, see the Methodology section.
For a detailed explanation of indexes, refer to the individual index section.

WHERE IDAHO RANKS – MEASURE BY MEASURE

		50th	40th	30th	20th	10th	1st

ECONOMIC PERFORMANCE INDEX MEASURES

Employment
- Long-Term Employment Growth (10)
- Short-Term Employment Growth (9)
- Unemployment Rate (21)
- Unemployment Duration (2)

Earnings & Job Quality
- Average Annual Pay (44)
- Average Annual Pay Growth (29)
- Health Coverage (30)

Equity
- Poverty Rate (31)
- Income Distribution (15)
- Income Distribution Change (34)
- Rural/Urban Disparity (48)

Environmental, Social & Health Conditions
- Air Quality (1)
- Superfund Dumpsites (42)
- Hazardous Waste Generation (46)
- Surface Water Discharge (21)
- Infant Mortality (24)
- Crime Rate (10)
- Teen Pregnancy (19)
- Heart Disease (8)
- Cancer Cases (7)
- Infectious Diseases (14)

BUSINESS VITALITY INDEX MEASURES

Competitiveness of Existing Business
- Traded Sector Strength (21)
- Change in Traded Sector Strength (14)
- Business Closings (31)
- Manufacturing Capital Investment (3)

Entrepreneurial Energy
- New Companies (3)
- Change in New Companies (6)
- New Business Job Growth (18)

Structural Diversity
- Sectoral Diversity (41)
- Dynamic Diversity (36)

DEVELOPMENT CAPACITY INDEX MEASURES

Human Resources
- High School Graduation (12)
- High School Education Attainment (19)
- College Education Attainment (36)

Technology Resources
- Ph.D. Scientists & Engineers in Workforce (16)
- Science/Engineering Graduate Students (26)
- Patents Issued (14)
- University Research & Development (43)
- Federal Research & Development (10)
- SBIR Grants (41)

Financial Resources
- Commercial Bank Deposits (40)
- Loans to Deposits (8)
- Loans to Equity (2)
- Commercial & Industrial Loans (21)
- Comm. & Ind. Loans to Total Loans (30)
- Venture Capital Investments (37)
- SBIC Financings (44)

Infrastructure & Amenity Resources
- Highway Deficiency (45)
- Bridge Deficiency (8)
- Urban Mass Transit Availability (48)
- Energy Cost (2)
- Sewage Treatment Needs (17)
- Urban Housing Costs (18)
- Health Professional Shortage Areas (41)
- Tourism Spending (20)

TAX & FISCAL SYSTEM INDEX MEASURES

- Total Tax & Fiscal System Score (2)
- Fiscal Stability & Balanced Revenue (15)
- Tax Fairness (4)
- Fiscal Equalization (6)

	50th	40th	30th	20th	10th	1st

ILLINOIS 1994 REPORT CARD

ECONOMIC PERFORMANCE	D
Employment ....D	
Earnings & Job Quality ....A	
Equity ....F	

BUSINESS VITALITY	A
Business Competitiveness ....B	
Entrepreneurial Energy C	
Structural Diversity ....A	

DEVELOPMENT CAPACITY	A
Human Resources ....B	
Technology Resources ....B	
Financial Resources ....A	
Infrastructure & Amenity Resources.....................A	

Tax & Fiscal System	√

- **Economic Performance:** Illinois has great jobs if you can get one. Its short-term employment growth and unemployment rate and duration all rank very low, while average annual pay and pay growth are both top ten.

- **Business Vitality:** Even though not everyone is benefiting yet, Illinois businesses are robust. New companies are highest in the nation, business closings are low, the traded sector is strong, and the economy is diverse. New business job growth has not caught up.

- **Development Capacity:** All of the state's resources are as strong as its businesses are vital, boding well for the future. The workforce is educated, technology resources are high, the physical infrastructure is good, and financial resources are particularly strong led by the third highest rate of commercial & industrial loans and SBIC financings.

Five Year Grade Trends

Key	
Economic Performance	———
Business Vitality	▒▒▒▒▒
Development Capacity	– – –

For more information on how grades and ranks are calculated, see the Methodology section.
For a detailed explanation of indexes, refer to the individual index section.

The Corporation for Enterprise Development

WHERE ILLINOIS RANKS – MEASURE BY MEASURE

| | 50th | 40th | 30th | 20th | 10th | 1st |

ECONOMIC PERFORMANCE INDEX MEASURES

Employment
- Long-Term Employment Growth (37)
- Short-Term Employment Growth (43)
- Unemployment Rate (38)
- Unemployment Duration (36)

Earnings & Job Quality
- Average Annual Pay (7)
- Average Annual Pay Growth (7)
- Health Coverage (27)

Equity
- Poverty Rate (33)
- Income Distribution (39)
- Income Distribution Change (20)
- Rural/Urban Disparity (45)

Environmental, Social & Health Conditions
- Air Quality (44)
- Superfund Dumpsites (10)
- Hazardous Waste Generation (39)
- Surface Water Discharge (35)
- Infant Mortality (39)
- Crime Rate (34)
- Teen Pregnancy (32)
- Heart Disease (37)
- Cancer Cases (28)
- Infectious Diseases (29)

BUSINESS VITALITY INDEX MEASURES

Competitiveness of Existing Business
- Traded Sector Strength (10)
- Change in Traded Sector Strength (25)
- Business Closings (9)
- Manufacturing Capital Investment (32)

Entrepreneurial Energy
- New Companies (35)
- Change in New Companies (1)
- New Business Job Growth (46)

Structural Diversity
- Sectoral Diversity (9)
- Dynamic Diversity (21)

DEVELOPMENT CAPACITY INDEX MEASURES

Human Resources
- High School Graduation (18)
- High School Education Attainment (24)
- College Education Attainment (14)

Technology Resources
- Ph.D. Scientists & Engineers in Workforce (26)
- Science/Engineering Graduate Students (13)
- Patents Issued (9)
- University Research & Development (29)
- Federal Research & Development (32)
- SBIR Grants (27)

Financial Resources
- Commercial Bank Deposits (5)
- Loans to Deposits (27)
- Loans to Equity (38)
- Commercial & Industrial Loans (5)
- Comm. & Ind. Loans to Total Loans (3)
- Venture Capital Investments (17)
- SBIC Financings (3)

Infrastructure & Amenity Resources
- Highway Deficiency (22)
- Bridge Deficiency (14)
- Urban Mass Transit Availability (3)
- Energy Cost (37)
- Sewage Treatment Needs (23)
- Urban Housing Costs (24)
- Health Professional Shortage Areas (20)
- Tourism Spending (24)

TAX & FISCAL SYSTEM INDEX MEASURES

- Total Tax & Fiscal System Score (35)
- Fiscal Stability & Balanced Revenue (39)
- Tax Fairness (16)
- Fiscal Equalization (36)

| | 50th | 40th | 30th | 20th | 10th | 1st |

INDIANA 1994 REPORT CARD

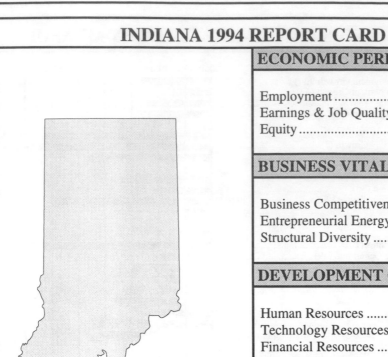

ECONOMIC PERFORMANCE	A
Employment	A
Earnings & Job Quality	B
Equity	B

BUSINESS VITALITY	A
Business Competitiveness	A
Entrepreneurial Energy	C
Structural Diversity	B

DEVELOPMENT CAPACITY	D
Human Resources	D
Technology Resources	D
Financial Resources	C
Infrastructure & Amenity Resources	C

Tax & Fiscal System	–

- **Economic Performance:** Indiana showed improvement in all aspects of economic performance as the state's grade jumped from a C to an A. Most noticeable was a jump to the nation's second best short-term employment growth rate, which improved job opportunity to the nation's sixth best. Also, ranks in health coverage improved and relative poverty decreased.

- **Business Vitality:** As a result of continued strength in the competitiveness of the state's firms, as well as improved entrepreneurial energy (new firm growth and new business job growth), Indiana's vitality improved to second best in the nation.

- **Development Capacity:** Indiana's development resources are the weakest in the region. With the nation's fourth lowest college attainment, human resources are below average, as are the state's technology resources. The state's financial and infrastructure resources are only average.

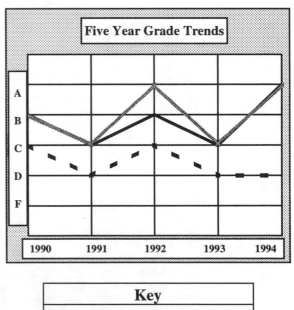

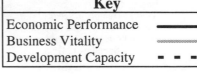

For more information on how grades and ranks are calculated, see the Methodology section.
For a detailed explanation of indexes, refer to the individual index section.

The Corporation for Enterprise Development

WHERE INDIANA RANKS – MEASURE BY MEASURE

ECONOMIC PERFORMANCE INDEX MEASURES

| | | 50th | 40th | 30th | 20th | 10th | 1st |

Employment
Long-Term Employment Growth (31)....................
Short-Term Employment Growth (2) ....
Unemployment Rate (13)....................................
Unemployment Duration (12) ....

Earnings &
Job Quality
Average Annual Pay (23) ....
Average Annual Pay Growth (33) ....
Health Coverage (9) ....

Equity
Poverty Rate (20) ....
Income Distribution (23).....................................
Income Distribution Change (36).........................
Rural/Urban Disparity (10) ....

Environmental,
Social &
Health
Conditions
Air Quality (29)..
Superfund Dumpsites (30) ....
Hazardous Waste Generation (31).......................
Surface Water Discharge (48) ....
Infant Mortality (36) ....
Crime Rate (20)..
Teen Pregnancy (29) ....
Heart Disease (34)..
Cancer Cases (29)..
Infectious Diseases (10) ....

BUSINESS VITALITY INDEX MEASURES

Competitiveness
of Existing
Business
Traded Sector Strength (9) ....
Change in Traded Sector Strength (16)..................
Business Closings (8)...
Manufacturing Capital Investment (13) ....

Entrepreneurial
Energy
New Companies (41)..
Change in New Companies (19) ....
New Business Job Growth (24) ....

Structural
Diversity
Sectoral Diversity (20) ....
Dynamic Diversity (14).......................................

DEVELOPMENT CAPACITY INDEX MEASURES

Human
Resources
High School Graduation (25) ....
High School Education Attainment (39)..................
College Education Attainment (47).......................

Technology
Resources
Ph.D. Scientists & Engineers in Workforce (46).....
Science/Engineering Graduate Students (18)..........
Patents Issued (25) ....
University Research & Development (39)................
Federal Research & Development (38)...................
SBIR Grants (43)..

Financial
Resources
Commercial Bank Deposits (28) ....
Loans to Deposits (25) ....
Loans to Equity (24)..
Commercial & Industrial Loans (28).....................
Comm. & Ind. Loans to Total Loans (28) ....
Venture Capital Investments (4)...........................
SBIC Financings (26)..

Infrastructure
& Amenity
Resources
Highway Deficiency (42) ....
Bridge Deficiency (24).......................................
Urban Mass Transit Availability (31)....................
Energy Cost (13) ....
Sewage Treatment Needs (31)............................
Urban Housing Costs (6).....................................
Health Professional Shortage Areas (22)................
Tourism Spending (47) ....

TAX & FISCAL SYSTEM INDEX MEASURES

Total Tax & Fiscal System Score (40).....................
Fiscal Stability & Balanced Revenue (18)...............
Tax Fairness (45)..
Fiscal Equalization (26) ....

| | | 50th | 40th | 30th | 20th | 10th | 1st |

IOWA 1994 REPORT CARD

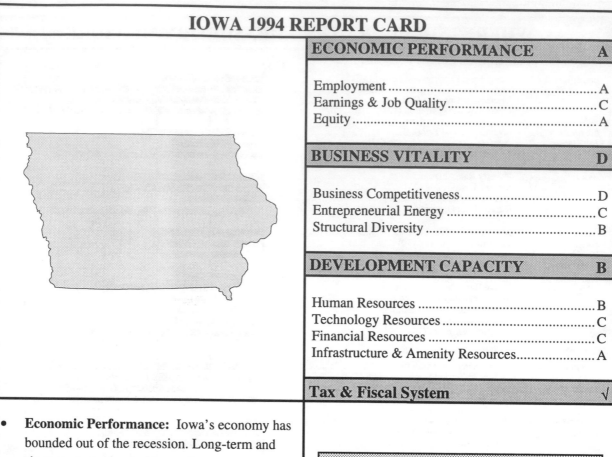

ECONOMIC PERFORMANCE	A
Employment	A
Earnings & Job Quality	C
Equity	A

BUSINESS VITALITY	D
Business Competitiveness	D
Entrepreneurial Energy	C
Structural Diversity	B

DEVELOPMENT CAPACITY	B
Human Resources	B
Technology Resources	C
Financial Resources	C
Infrastructure & Amenity Resources	A

Tax & Fiscal System	√

- **Economic Performance:** Iowa's economy has bounded out of the recession. Long-term and short-term employment growth are way up, accompanied by low short-term unemployment. Even low annual pay shows positive signs as Iowa ranked 11th in pay growth. All this has helped to give the state the nation's best equity ranking.

- **Business Vitality:** Iowa's growing economy is not very dynamic. There were few new companies (despite high employment growth), and business closings were low. In addition, the traded sector appears to be weakening and manufacturing capital investment is low.

- **Development Capacity:** Iowa's loan activity is very low which may explain the lack of business dynamism. The rest of the state's resources are strong, with good high school graduation and attainment rates, and a rank of seven for infrastructure and amenities, lead by the 6th best highways and the lowest sewage needs.

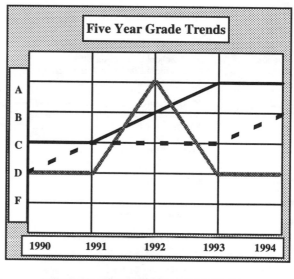

Five Year Grade Trends

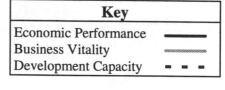

Key	
Economic Performance	——————
Business Vitality	≈≈≈≈≈≈
Development Capacity	- - -

For more information on how grades and ranks are calculated, see the Methodology section.
For a detailed explanation of indexes, refer to the individual index section.

WHERE IOWA RANKS – MEASURE BY MEASURE

Scale across top: 50th 40th 30th 20th 10th 1st

ECONOMIC PERFORMANCE INDEX MEASURES

Employment
- Long-Term Employment Growth (19)
- Short-Term Employment Growth (7)
- Unemployment Rate (4)
- Unemployment Duration (4)

Earnings & Job Quality
- Average Annual Pay (43)
- Average Annual Pay Growth (11)
- Health Coverage (17)

Equity
- Poverty Rate (17)
- Income Distribution (2)
- Income Distribution Change (7)
- Rural/Urban Disparity (17)

Environmental, Social & Health Conditions
- Air Quality (1)
- Superfund Dumpsites (34)
- Hazardous Waste Generation (16)
- Surface Water Discharge (32)
- Infant Mortality (6)
- Crime Rate (9)
- Teen Pregnancy (9)
- Heart Disease (17)
- Cancer Cases (36)
- Infectious Diseases (3)

BUSINESS VITALITY INDEX MEASURES

Competitiveness of Existing Business
- Traded Sector Strength (30)
- Change in Traded Sector Strength (45)
- Business Closings (14)
- Manufacturing Capital Investment (37)

Entrepreneurial Energy
- New Companies (47)
- Change in New Companies (34)
- New Business Job Growth (8)

Structural Diversity
- Sectoral Diversity (38)
- Dynamic Diversity (10)

DEVELOPMENT CAPACITY INDEX MEASURES

Human Resources
- High School Graduation (4)
- High School Education Attainment (16)
- College Education Attainment (39)

Technology Resources
- Ph.D. Scientists & Engineers in Workforce (42)
- Science/Engineering Graduate Students (12)
- Patents Issued (30)
- University Research & Development (7)
- Federal Research & Development (33)
- SBIR Grants (37)

Financial Resources
- Commercial Bank Deposits (6)
- Loans to Deposits (40)
- Loans to Equity (40)
- Commercial & Industrial Loans (29)
- Comm. & Ind. Loans to Total Loans (37)
- Venture Capital Investments (32)
- SBIC Financings (33)

Infrastructure & Amenity Resources
- Highway Deficiency (6)
- Bridge Deficiency (23)
- Urban Mass Transit Availability (34)
- Energy Cost (19)
- Sewage Treatment Needs (1)
- Urban Housing Costs (15)
- Health Professional Shortage Areas (24)
- Tourism Spending (37)

TAX & FISCAL SYSTEM INDEX MEASURES

- Total Tax & Fiscal System Score (22)
- Fiscal Stability & Balanced Revenue (23)
- Tax Fairness (37)
- Fiscal Equalization (17)

Scale across bottom: 50th 40th 30th 20th 10th 1st

KANSAS 1994 REPORT CARD

ECONOMIC PERFORMANCE — C

Employment C
Earnings & Job Quality C
Equity C

BUSINESS VITALITY — B

Business Competitiveness C
Entrepreneurial Energy .... B
Structural Diversity .... B

DEVELOPMENT CAPACITY — C

Human Resources .... A
Technology Resources .... D
Financial Resources .... D
Infrastructure & Amenity Resources C

Tax & Fiscal System — +

- **Economic Performance:** The Kansas economy is maintaining course. Although short- and long-term employment growth were poor, unemployment was ninth lowest in the nation and eight shortest. Poverty was low and the gap between rich and poor eleventh smallest in the country. Health coverage is good, but the relatively low annual pay needs improvement.

- **Business Vitality:** The Kansas business community is growing: change in new companies was thirteenth best while business closings were low. The economy is diverse as well. Only low manufacturing capital investment drags down Kansas's Vitality grade.

- **Development Capacity:** Kansas' development capacity is mixed. It ranks second in the nation in human resources. High school attainment was fifth and college attainment eleventh. But the state is weak in technology and financial resources, with little federal R&D, few SBIR grants and very low loans to deposits and equity.

Five Year Grade Trends

	1990	1991	1992	1993	1994

Key

Economic Performance	————
Business Vitality	————
Development Capacity	- - -

For more information on how grades and ranks are calculated, see the Methodology section.
For a detailed explanation of indexes, refer to the individual index section.

WHERE KANSAS RANKS – MEASURE BY MEASURE

50th 40th 30th 20th 10th 1st

ECONOMIC PERFORMANCE INDEX MEASURES

Employment
Long-Term Employment Growth (39)
Short-Term Employment Growth (42)
Unemployment Rate (9)
Unemployment Duration (8)

Earnings & Job Quality
Average Annual Pay (35)
Average Annual Pay Growth (33)
Health Coverage (19)

Equity
Poverty Rate (14)
Income Distribution (11)
Income Distribution Change (38)
Rural/Urban Disparity (39)

Environmental, Social & Health Conditions
Air Quality (1)
Superfund Dumpsites (19)
Hazardous Waste Generation (41)
Surface Water Discharge (44)
Infant Mortality (24)
Crime Rate (29)
Teen Pregnancy (23)
Heart Disease (14)
Cancer Cases (21)
Infectious Diseases (11)

BUSINESS VITALITY INDEX MEASURES

Competitiveness of Existing Business
Traded Sector Strength (31)
Change in Traded Sector Strength (30)
Business Closings (17)
Manufacturing Capital Investment (44)

Entrepreneurial Energy
New Companies (32)
Change in New Companies (13)
New Business Job Growth (21)

Structural Diversity
Sectoral Diversity (33)
Dynamic Diversity (6)

DEVELOPMENT CAPACITY INDEX MEASURES

Human Resources
High School Graduation (10)
High School Education Attainment (5)
College Education Attainment (11)

Technology Resources
Ph.D. Scientists & Engineers in Workforce (43)
Science/Engineering Graduate Students (8)
Patents Issued (33)
University Research & Development (34)
Federal Research & Development (48)
SBIR Grants (45)

Financial Resources
Commercial Bank Deposits (13)
Loans to Deposits (45)
Loans to Equity (44)
Commercial & Industrial Loans (35)
Comm. & Ind. Loans to Total Loans (25)
Venture Capital Investments (24)
SBIC Financings (34)

Infrastructure & Amenity Resources
Highway Deficiency (29)
Bridge Deficiency (30)
Urban Mass Transit Availability (43)
Energy Cost (28)
Sewage Treatment Needs (18)
Urban Housing Costs (3)
Health Professional Shortage Areas (7)
Tourism Spending (40)

TAX & FISCAL SYSTEM INDEX MEASURES

Total Tax & Fiscal System Score (13)
Fiscal Stability & Balanced Revenue (8)
Tax Fairness (15)
Fiscal Equalization (28)

50th 40th 30th 20th 10th 1st

KENTUCKY 1994 REPORT CARD

ECONOMIC PERFORMANCE — F

Employment C
Earnings & Job Quality C
Equity .... F

BUSINESS VITALITY — C

Business Competitiveness C
Entrepreneurial Energy .... D
Structural Diversity .... A

DEVELOPMENT CAPACITY — F

Human Resources .... D
Technology Resources .... F
Financial Resources C
Infrastructure & Amenity Resources .... B

Tax & Fiscal System — √

- **Economic Performance:** Led by modest improvements in relative short-term employment growth and pay growth, Kentucky's employment and job quality rankings improved. However, with the persistence of a high poverty rate and poor income distribution, Kentucky continues to receive a failing grade.

- **Business Vitality:** Despite continued strength in structural diversity of businesses, Kentucky dropped one letter grade as entrepreneurial energy weakened, marked by a sharp drop in change in new company formations.

- **Development Capacity:** Kentucky's development resources continue to be among the weakest in the nation, marked by the second worst technology resources in the nation and very low high school and college education attainment. However, one strength is the state's strong infrastructure resources, led by good highways and the nation's fourth lowest energy costs.

Five Year Grade Trends

| | 1990 | 1991 | 1992 | 1993 | 1994 |

Key
Economic Performance ———
Business Vitality ———
Development Capacity - - -

For more information on how grades and ranks are calculated, see the Methodology section.
For a detailed explanation of indexes, refer to the individual index section.

WHERE KENTUCKY RANKS – MEASURE BY MEASURE

ECONOMIC PERFORMANCE INDEX MEASURES

Category	Measure	50th	40th	30th	20th	10th	1st

Employment
- Long-Term Employment Growth (32)
- Short-Term Employment Growth (17)
- Unemployment Rate (22)
- Unemployment Duration (43)

Earnings & Job Quality
- Average Annual Pay (37)
- Average Annual Pay Growth (17)
- Health Coverage (32)

Equity
- Poverty Rate (46)
- Income Distribution (48)
- Income Distribution Change (47)
- Rural/Urban Disparity (11)

Environmental, Social & Health Conditions
- Air Quality (20)
- Superfund Dumpsites (28)
- Hazardous Waste Generation (23)
- Surface Water Discharge (40)
- Infant Mortality (28)
- Crime Rate (5)
- Teen Pregnancy (34)
- Heart Disease (47)
- Cancer Cases (43)
- Infectious Diseases (16)

BUSINESS VITALITY INDEX MEASURES

Competitiveness of Existing Business
- Traded Sector Strength (24)
- Change in Traded Sector Strength (19)
- Business Closings (30)
- Manufacturing Capital Investment (22)

Entrepreneurial Energy
- New Companies (42)
- Change in New Companies (38)
- New Business Job Growth (27)

Structural Diversity
- Sectoral Diversity (10)
- Dynamic Diversity (9)

DEVELOPMENT CAPACITY INDEX MEASURES

Human Resources
- High School Graduation (36)
- High School Education Attainment (46)
- College Education Attainment (44)

Technology Resources
- Ph.D. Scientists & Engineers in Workforce (47)
- Science/Engineering Graduate Students (47)
- Patents Issued (44)
- University Research & Development (47)
- Federal Research & Development (49)
- SBIR Grants (46)

Financial Resources
- Commercial Bank Deposits (19)
- Loans to Deposits (20)
- Loans to Equity (25)
- Commercial & Industrial Loans (20)
- Comm. & Ind. Loans to Total Loans (33)
- Venture Capital Investments (25)
- SBIC Financings (43)

Infrastructure & Amenity Resources
- Highway Deficiency (17)
- Bridge Deficiency (31)
- Urban Mass Transit Availability (29)
- Energy Cost (4)
- Sewage Treatment Needs (34)
- Urban Housing Costs (4)
- Health Professional Shortage Areas (34)
- Tourism Spending (33)

TAX & FISCAL SYSTEM INDEX MEASURES

- Total Tax & Fiscal System Score (17)
- Fiscal Stability & Balanced Revenue (24)
- Tax Fairness (32)
- Fiscal Equalization (10)

LOUISIANA 1994 REPORT CARD

ECONOMIC PERFORMANCE	F

Employment .... F
Earnings & Job Quality .... D
Equity .... D

BUSINESS VITALITY	C

Business Competitiveness C
Entrepreneurial Energy .... B
Structural Diversity C

DEVELOPMENT CAPACITY	F

Human Resources .... F
Technology Resources .... D
Financial Resources .... F
Infrastructure & Amenity Resources .... D

Tax & Fiscal System	–

- **Economic Performance:** With poor employment growth, poor job quality and the least equitable distribution of income in the country, Louisiana's economy ranks last in the nation on economic performance. One positive trend is the change in income distribution, which jumped from a rank of 40th last year to 13th this year.

- **Business Vitality:** Led by strong manufacturing capital investment and new business job growth, Louisiana's vitality, though still only average, has improved one grade in each of the last two years.

- **Development Capacity:** Louisiana's development resources are the second worst in the country. Both human resources, with the nation's lowest ranking for high school graduation, and financial resources receive failing marks, while technology and infrastructure resources are only slightly better.

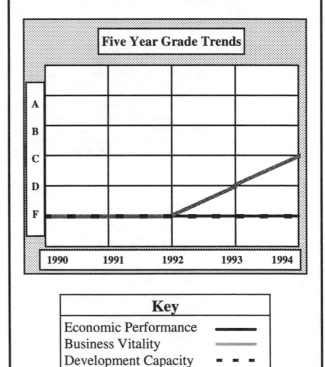

For more information on how grades and ranks are calculated, see the Methodology section.
For a detailed explanation of indexes, refer to the individual index section.

WHERE LOUISIANA RANKS – MEASURE BY MEASURE

ECONOMIC PERFORMANCE INDEX MEASURES

Employment
- Long-Term Employment Growth (47)
- Short-Term Employment Growth (49)
- Unemployment Rate (38)
- Unemployment Duration (29)

Earnings & Job Quality
- Average Annual Pay (31)
- Average Annual Pay Growth (43)
- Health Coverage (50)

Equity
- Poverty Rate (49)
- Income Distribution (50)
- Income Distribution Change (13)
- Rural/Urban Disparity (20)

Environmental, Social & Health Conditions
- Air Quality (17)
- Superfund Dumpsites (7)
- Hazardous Waste Generation (49)
- Surface Water Discharge (39)
- Infant Mortality (36)
- Crime Rate (46)
- Teen Pregnancy (43)
- Heart Disease (48)
- Cancer Cases (22)
- Infectious Diseases (28)

BUSINESS VITALITY INDEX MEASURES

Competitiveness of Existing Business
- Traded Sector Strength (43)
- Change in Traded Sector Strength (38)
- Business Closings (20)
- Manufacturing Capital Investment (4)

Entrepreneurial Energy
- New Companies (37)
- Change in New Companies (18)
- New Business Job Growth (13)

Structural Diversity
- Sectoral Diversity (25)
- Dynamic Diversity (38)

DEVELOPMENT CAPACITY INDEX MEASURES

Human Resources
- High School Graduation (50)
- High School Education Attainment (45)
- College Education Attainment (39)

Technology Resources
- Ph.D. Scientists & Engineers in Workforce (36)
- Science/Engineering Graduate Students (34)
- Patents Issued (36)
- University Research & Development (33)
- Federal Research & Development (46)
- SBIR Grants (44)

Financial Resources
- Commercial Bank Deposits (38)
- Loans to Deposits (50)
- Loans to Equity (47)
- Commercial & Industrial Loans (43)
- Comm. & Ind. Loans to Total Loans (26)
- Venture Capital Investments (37)
- SBIC Financings (14)

Infrastructure & Amenity Resources
- Highway Deficiency (48)
- Bridge Deficiency (39)
- Urban Mass Transit Availability (23)
- Energy Cost (20)
- Sewage Treatment Needs (27)
- Urban Housing Costs (28)
- Health Professional Shortage Areas (48)
- Tourism Spending (28)

TAX & FISCAL SYSTEM INDEX MEASURES

- Total Tax & Fiscal System Score (36)
- Fiscal Stability & Balanced Revenue (38)
- Tax Fairness (39)
- Fiscal Equalization (13)

Chart scale: 50th, 40th, 30th, 20th, 10th, 1st

MAINE 1994 REPORT CARD

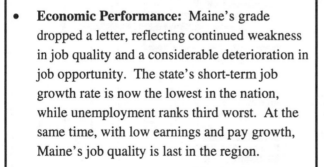

ECONOMIC PERFORMANCE	D
Employment	F
Earnings & Job Quality	D
Equity	B

BUSINESS VITALITY	B
Business Competitiveness	C
Entrepreneurial Energy	B
Structural Diversity	B

DEVELOPMENT CAPACITY	D
Human Resources	C
Technology Resources	F
Financial Resources	B
Infrastructure & Amenity Resources	F

Tax & Fiscal System	+

- **Economic Performance:** Maine's grade dropped a letter, reflecting continued weakness in job quality and a considerable deterioration in job opportunity. The state's short-term job growth rate is now the lowest in the nation, while unemployment ranks third worst. At the same time, with low earnings and pay growth, Maine's job quality is last in the region.

- **Business Vitality:** Maine's above average grade reflects a fairly well-diversified economy combined with strong entrepreneurial energy, especially in the growth of new firms. A weak traded sector remains a drag on the economy.

- **Development Capacity:** Maine is the only state in the region whose development resources earn less than a C. The state's infrastructure and technology resources both receive failing marks. However, the state's financial resources are above average and the high school graduation rate is in the top fifteen.

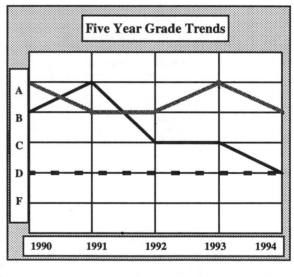

Five Year Grade Trends

| | 1990 | 1991 | 1992 | 1993 | 1994 |

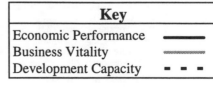

Key

Economic Performance ──────

Business Vitality ════════

Development Capacity ▬ ▬ ▬

For more information on how grades and ranks are calculated, see the Methodology section.
For a detailed explanation of indexes, refer to the individual index section.

WHERE MAINE RANKS – MEASURE BY MEASURE

		50th	40th	30th	20th	10th	1st

ECONOMIC PERFORMANCE INDEX MEASURES

Category	Measure (rank)
Employment	Long-Term Employment Growth (30)
	Short-Term Employment Growth (50)
	Unemployment Rate (48)
	Unemployment Duration (41)
Earnings & Job Quality	Average Annual Pay (38)
	Average Annual Pay Growth (37)
	Health Coverage (26)
Equity	Poverty Rate (26)
	Income Distribution (26)
	Income Distribution Change (41)
	Rural/Urban Disparity (1)
Environmental, Social & Health Conditions	Air Quality (34)
	Superfund Dumpsites (37)
	Hazardous Waste Generation (5)
	Surface Water Discharge (13)
	Infant Mortality (2)
	Crime Rate (8)
	Teen Pregnancy (10)
	Heart Disease (28)
	Cancer Cases (45)
	Infectious Diseases (2)

BUSINESS VITALITY INDEX MEASURES

Category	Measure (rank)
Competitiveness of Existing Business	Traded Sector Strength (45)
	Change in Traded Sector Strength (50)
	Business Closings (7)
	Manufacturing Capital Investment (19)
Entrepreneurial Energy	New Companies (16)
	Change in New Companies (7)
	New Business Job Growth (45)
Structural Diversity	Sectoral Diversity (30)
	Dynamic Diversity (8)

DEVELOPMENT CAPACITY INDEX MEASURES

Category	Measure (rank)
Human Resources	High School Graduation (14)
	High School Education Attainment (19)
	College Education Attainment (39)
Technology Resources	Ph.D. Scientists & Engineers in Workforce (30)
	Science/Engineering Graduate Students (49)
	Patents Issued (40)
	University Research & Development (50)
	Federal Research & Development (44)
	SBIR Grants (33)
Financial Resources	Commercial Bank Deposits (49)
	Loans to Deposits (14)
	Loans to Equity (4)
	Commercial & Industrial Loans (34)
	Comm. & Ind. Loans to Total Loans (16)
	Venture Capital Investments (37)
	SBIC Financings (6)
Infrastructure & Amenity Resources	Highway Deficiency (44)
	Bridge Deficiency (37)
	Urban Mass Transit Availability (41)
	Energy Cost (41)
	Sewage Treatment Needs (29)
	Urban Housing Costs (43)
	Health Professional Shortage Areas (14)
	Tourism Spending (31)

TAX & FISCAL SYSTEM INDEX MEASURES

	Measure (rank)
	Total Tax & Fiscal System Score (6)
	Fiscal Stability & Balanced Revenue (32)
	Tax Fairness (3)
	Fiscal Equalization (34)

		50th	40th	30th	20th	10th	1st

MARYLAND 1994 REPORT CARD

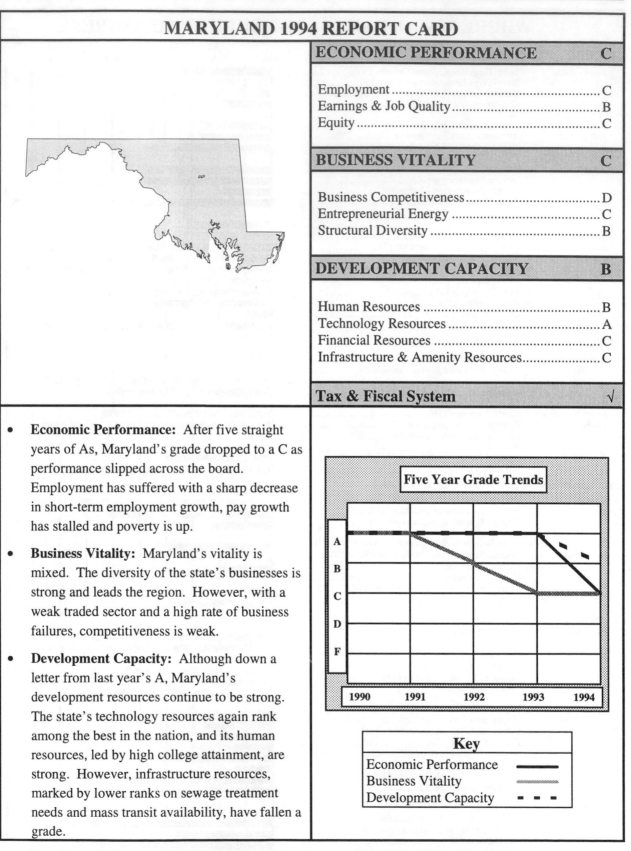

ECONOMIC PERFORMANCE	C
Employment	C
Earnings & Job Quality	B
Equity	C

BUSINESS VITALITY	C
Business Competitiveness	D
Entrepreneurial Energy	C
Structural Diversity	B

DEVELOPMENT CAPACITY	B
Human Resources	B
Technology Resources	A
Financial Resources	C
Infrastructure & Amenity Resources	C

Tax & Fiscal System	√

- **Economic Performance:** After five straight years of As, Maryland's grade dropped to a C as performance slipped across the board. Employment has suffered with a sharp decrease in short-term employment growth, pay growth has stalled and poverty is up.

- **Business Vitality:** Maryland's vitality is mixed. The diversity of the state's businesses is strong and leads the region. However, with a weak traded sector and a high rate of business failures, competitiveness is weak.

- **Development Capacity:** Although down a letter from last year's A, Maryland's development resources continue to be strong. The state's technology resources again rank among the best in the nation, and its human resources, led by high college attainment, are strong. However, infrastructure resources, marked by lower ranks on sewage treatment needs and mass transit availability, have fallen a grade.

Five Year Grade Trends

Key	
Economic Performance	———
Business Vitality	———
Development Capacity	- - -

For more information on how grades and ranks are calculated, see the Methodology section.
For a detailed explanation of indexes, refer to the individual index section.

WHERE MARYLAND RANKS – MEASURE BY MEASURE

50th   40th   30th   20th   10th   1st

ECONOMIC PERFORMANCE INDEX MEASURES

Employment
Long-Term Employment Growth (15)..................
Short-Term Employment Growth (40) ....
Unemployment Rate (22) ....
Unemployment Duration (44) ....

Earnings & Job Quality
Average Annual Pay (9) ....
Average Annual Pay Growth (35) ....
Health Coverage (12) ....

Equity
Poverty Rate (19) ....
Income Distribution (19)........................
Income Distribution Change (38)..................
Rural/Urban Disparity (39) ....

Environmental, Social & Health Conditions
Air Quality (46)............................
Superfund Dumpsites (6) ....
Hazardous Waste Generation (9).................
Surface Water Discharge (24) ....
Infant Mortality (32) ....
Crime Rate (43)...............................
Teen Pregnancy (19) ....
Heart Disease (25)............................
Cancer Cases (19) ....
Infectious Diseases (39) ....

BUSINESS VITALITY INDEX MEASURES

Competitiveness of Existing Business
Traded Sector Strength (41) ....
Change in Traded Sector Strength (35)............
Business Closings (38)..........................
Manufacturing Capital Investment (21) ....

Entrepreneurial Energy
New Companies (10)............................
Change in New Companies (28) ....
New Business Job Growth (34)...................

Structural Diversity
Sectoral Diversity (17) ....
Dynamic Diversity (15)..........................

DEVELOPMENT CAPACITY INDEX MEASURES

Human Resources
High School Graduation (28) ....
High School Education Attainment (24)..............
College Education Attainment (7)..................

Technology Resources
Ph.D. Scientists & Engineers in Workforce (3).......
Science/Engineering Graduate Students (19)..........
Patents Issued (21) ....
University Research & Development (1).................
Federal Research & Development (2)....................
SBIR Grants (6)...............................

Financial Resources
Commercial Bank Deposits (33) ....
Loans to Deposits (30) ....
Loans to Equity (21)............................
Commercial & Industrial Loans (37)...............
Comm. & Ind. Loans to Total Loans (36) ....
Venture Capital Investments (13).................
SBIC Financings (13)...........................

Infrastructure & Amenity Resources
Highway Deficiency (13) ....
Bridge Deficiency (29)..........................
Urban Mass Transit Availability (12)..............
Energy Cost (33) ....
Sewage Treatment Needs (30).....................
Urban Housing Costs (36).......................
Health Professional Shortage Areas (2)..................
Tourism Spending (38) ....

TAX & FISCAL SYSTEM INDEX MEASURES

Total Tax & Fiscal System Score (25)..................
Fiscal Stability & Balanced Revenue (28)..............
Tax Fairness (13)..............................
Fiscal Equalization (37) ....

50th   40th   30th   20th   10th   1st

MASSACHUSETTS 1994 REPORT CARD

ECONOMIC PERFORMANCE	C
Employment	D
Earnings & Job Quality	A
Equity	D

BUSINESS VITALITY	C
Business Competitiveness	A
Entrepreneurial Energy	D
Structural Diversity	C

DEVELOPMENT CAPACITY	A
Human Resources	A
Technology Resources	A
Financial Resources	A
Infrastructure & Amenity Resources	D

Tax & Fiscal System	√

- **Economic Performance:** Massachusetts has strong job quality, but poor job opportunity. While average pay is fifth in the nation and growing strong, long-term unemployment is poor and unemployment duration is the nation's second worst. Also, Massachusetts ranks last in the Northeast on measures of equity.

- **Business Vitality:** Entrepreneurial energy continues to be weak in Massachusetts, with few new companies and slow new business job growth. However, led by a robust traded sector, businesses remain competitive.

- **Development Capacity:** The state's development resources are among the nation's top five, leaving the state well positioned for an economic turnaround. Technology resources are the nation's best, and human and financial resources both rank second in the nation. Infrastructure resources continue to be the state's main weakness.

Five Year Grade Trends

Key	
Economic Performance	———
Business Vitality	———
Development Capacity	- - -

For more information on how grades and ranks are calculated, see the Methodology section.
For a detailed explanation of indexes, refer to the individual index section.

The Corporation for Enterprise Development

WHERE MASSACHUSETTS RANKS – MEASURE BY MEASURE

50th 40th 30th 20th 10th 1st

ECONOMIC PERFORMANCE INDEX MEASURES

Employment
- Long-Term Employment Growth (45)
- Short-Term Employment Growth (19)
- Unemployment Rate (31)
- Unemployment Duration (49)

Earnings & Job Quality
- Average Annual Pay (5)
- Average Annual Pay Growth (9)
- Health Coverage (8)

Equity
- Poverty Rate (6)
- Income Distribution (36)
- Income Distribution Change (44)
- Rural/Urban Disparity (46)

Environmental, Social & Health Conditions
- Air Quality (45)
- Superfund Dumpsites (25)
- Hazardous Waste Generation (21)
- Surface Water Discharge (18)
- Infant Mortality (5)
- Crime Rate (23)
- Teen Pregnancy (4)
- Heart Disease (20)
- Cancer Cases (39)
- Infectious Diseases (25)

BUSINESS VITALITY INDEX MEASURES

Competitiveness of Existing Business
- Traded Sector Strength (7)
- Change in Traded Sector Strength (8)
- Business Closings (11)
- Manufacturing Capital Investment (43)

Entrepreneurial Energy
- New Companies (44)
- Change in New Companies (25)
- New Business Job Growth (37)

Structural Diversity
- Sectoral Diversity (15)
- Dynamic Diversity (41)

DEVELOPMENT CAPACITY INDEX MEASURES

Human Resources
- High School Graduation (12)
- High School Education Attainment (13)
- College Education Attainment (1)

Technology Resources
- Ph.D. Scientists & Engineers in Workforce (4)
- Science/Engineering Graduate Students (1)
- Patents Issued (3)
- University Research & Development (2)
- Federal Research & Development (4)
- SBIR Grants (1)

Financial Resources
- Commercial Bank Deposits (17)
- Loans to Deposits (15)
- Loans to Equity (19)
- Commercial & Industrial Loans (7)
- Comm. & Ind. Loans to Total Loans (2)
- Venture Capital Investments (1)
- SBIC Financings (15)

Infrastructure & Amenity Resources
- Highway Deficiency (33)
- Bridge Deficiency (49)
- Urban Mass Transit Availability (4)
- Energy Cost (46)
- Sewage Treatment Needs (49)
- Urban Housing Costs (44)
- Health Professional Shortage Areas (13)
- Tourism Spending (39)

TAX & FISCAL SYSTEM INDEX MEASURES

- Total Tax & Fiscal System Score (26)
- Fiscal Stability & Balanced Revenue (20)
- Tax Fairness (26)
- Fiscal Equalization (32)

50th 40th 30th 20th 10th 1st

MICHIGAN 1994 REPORT CARD

ECONOMIC PERFORMANCE	C

Employment C
Earnings & Job Quality .... B
Equity .... D

BUSINESS VITALITY	C

Business Competitiveness .... A
Entrepreneurial Energy .... D
Structural Diversity C

DEVELOPMENT CAPACITY	C

Human Resources .... D
Technology Resources .... B
Financial Resources .... A
Infrastructure & Amenity Resources .... D

Tax & Fiscal System	√

- **Economic Performance:** Michigan's economy appears to have retrenched and pulled out of the recession. Short-term employment growth was very strong in an economy with already high pay. The only concern is that poor equity showings raise fears that not everyone is benefiting.

- **Business Vitality:** The state has made its existing businesses competitive but brought in few new ones. Michigan ranks fifth in traded sector strength (companies that compete out of state) and had few business closings. But it was second to last in new business formation.

- **Development Capacity:** Michigan has excellent financial and technological resources. It is top ten in patents issued, has many SBIR grants and science/engineering graduate students, coupled with aggressive loan activity, particularly commercial and industrial loans. The downside is a relatively uneducated populace and poor physical infrastructure.

Five Year Grade Trends

	1990	1991	1992	1993	1994
A					
B					
C					
D					
F					

Key

Economic Performance ———
Business Vitality ∼∼∼∼∼
Development Capacity ‑ ‑ ‑

For more information on how grades and ranks are calculated, see the Methodology section.
For a detailed explanation of indexes, refer to the individual index section.

WHERE MICHIGAN RANKS – MEASURE BY MEASURE

ECONOMIC PERFORMANCE INDEX MEASURES

Employment	Long-Term Employment Growth (28)
	Short-Term Employment Growth (11)
	Unemployment Rate (32)
	Unemployment Duration (32)
Earnings & Job Quality	Average Annual Pay (8)
	Average Annual Pay Growth (26)
	Health Coverage (15)
Equity	Poverty Rate (27)
	Income Distribution (35)
	Income Distribution Change (31)
	Rural/Urban Disparity (42)
Environmental, Social & Health Conditions	Air Quality (31)
	Superfund Dumpsites (38)
	Hazardous Waste Generation (44)
	Surface Water Discharge (46)
	Infant Mortality (40)
	Crime Rate (32)
	Teen Pregnancy (27)
	Heart Disease (42)
	Cancer Cases (18)
	Infectious Diseases (12)

BUSINESS VITALITY INDEX MEASURES

Competitiveness of Existing Business	Traded Sector Strength (5)
	Change in Traded Sector Strength (43)
	Business Closings (3)
	Manufacturing Capital Investment (15)
Entrepreneurial Energy	New Companies (49)
	Change in New Companies (37)
	New Business Job Growth (15)
Structural Diversity	Sectoral Diversity (45)
	Dynamic Diversity (18)

DEVELOPMENT CAPACITY INDEX MEASURES

Human Resources	High School Graduation (37)
	High School Education Attainment (24)
	College Education Attainment (36)
Technology Resources	Ph.D. Scientists & Engineers in Workforce (35)
	Science/Engineering Graduate Students (16)
	Patents Issued (7)
	University Research & Development (26)
	Federal Research & Development (31)
	SBIR Grants (17)
Financial Resources	Commercial Bank Deposits (32)
	Loans to Deposits (19)
	Loans to Equity (7)
	Commercial & Industrial Loans (11)
	Comm. & Ind. Loans to Total Loans (5)
	Venture Capital Investments (35)
	SBIC Financings (19)
Infrastructure & Amenity Resources	Highway Deficiency (37)
	Bridge Deficiency (28)
	Urban Mass Transit Availability (25)
	Energy Cost (36)
	Sewage Treatment Needs (36)
	Urban Housing Costs (19)
	Health Professional Shortage Areas (27)
	Tourism Spending (45)

TAX & FISCAL SYSTEM INDEX MEASURES

Total Tax & Fiscal System Score (31)
Fiscal Stability & Balanced Revenue (34)
Tax Fairness (18)
Fiscal Equalization (35)

MINNESOTA 1994 REPORT CARD

ECONOMIC PERFORMANCE	A
Employment	B
Earnings & Job Quality	B
Equity	B

BUSINESS VITALITY	B
Business Competitiveness	A
Entrepreneurial Energy	D
Structural Diversity	B

DEVELOPMENT CAPACITY	A
Human Resources	A
Technology Resources	B
Financial Resources	A
Infrastructure & Amenity Resources	A

Tax & Fiscal System	+

- **Economic Performance:** Up from last year's C, Minnesota earns its first A with the sixth best Economic Performance in the nation. Relative short- and long-term employment conditions improved dramatically, along with better income distribution in this state which already has well paying jobs.

- **Business Vitality:** Business Vitality is also up from a C to a B, from improvements in structural diversity and business competitiveness. Entrepreneurship remains low with a D. The high rate of business closings accompanied by few new companies indicates that the economy has little turnover.

- **Development Capacity:** Minnesota is tops in this index, rating at least a B in every subindex. It ranks second highest in infrastructure and amenities, third in financial resources, and fifth in human resources (with the country's best high school graduation rate). The state is strong in almost every single measure, with a median rank in only two of the twenty-five measures.

Five Year Grade Trends

	1990	1991	1992	1993	1994

Key
Economic Performance	——
Business Vitality	~~~~
Development Capacity	- - -

For more information on how grades and ranks are calculated, see the Methodology section.
For a detailed explanation of indexes, refer to the individual index section.

WHERE MINNESOTA RANKS – MEASURE BY MEASURE

ECONOMIC PERFORMANCE INDEX MEASURES

Employment
- Long-Term Employment Growth (27)
- Short-Term Employment Growth (23)
- Unemployment Rate (11)
- Unemployment Duration (18)

Earnings & Job Quality
- Average Annual Pay (14)
- Average Annual Pay Growth (13)
- Health Coverage (24)

Equity
- Poverty Rate (25)
- Income Distribution (10)
- Income Distribution Change (16)
- Rural/Urban Disparity (25)

Environmental, Social & Health Conditions
- Air Quality (19)
- Superfund Dumpsites (41)
- Hazardous Waste Generation (40)
- Surface Water Discharge (42)
- Infant Mortality (13)
- Crime Rate (17)
- Teen Pregnancy (3)
- Heart Disease (4)
- Cancer Cases (13)
- Infectious Diseases (8)

BUSINESS VITALITY INDEX MEASURES

Competitiveness of Existing Business
- Traded Sector Strength (12)
- Change in Traded Sector Strength (23)
- Business Closings (5)
- Manufacturing Capital Investment (28)

Entrepreneurial Energy
- New Companies (48)
- Change in New Companies (50)
- New Business Job Growth (4)

Structural Diversity
- Sectoral Diversity (18)
- Dynamic Diversity (24)

DEVELOPMENT CAPACITY INDEX MEASURES

Human Resources
- High School Graduation (1)
- High School Education Attainment (10)
- College Education Attainment (19)

Technology Resources
- Ph.D. Scientists & Engineers in Workforce (25)
- Science/Engineering Graduate Students (36)
- Patents Issued (5)
- University Research & Development (24)
- Federal Research & Development (25)
- SBIR Grants (21)

Financial Resources
- Commercial Bank Deposits (12)
- Loans to Deposits (16)
- Loans to Equity (13)
- Commercial & Industrial Loans (13)
- Comm. & Ind. Loans to Total Loans (19)
- Venture Capital Investments (6)
- SBIC Financings (5)

Infrastructure & Amenity Resources
- Highway Deficiency (3)
- Bridge Deficiency (5)
- Urban Mass Transit Availability (13)
- Energy Cost (12)
- Sewage Treatment Needs (15)
- Urban Housing Costs (31)
- Health Professional Shortage Areas (6)
- Tourism Spending (18)

TAX & FISCAL SYSTEM INDEX MEASURES
- Total Tax & Fiscal System Score (1)
- Fiscal Stability & Balanced Revenue (1)
- Tax Fairness (2)
- Fiscal Equalization (20)

MISSISSIPPI 1994 REPORT CARD

ECONOMIC PERFORMANCE — D

Employment .... B
Earnings & Job Quality .... F
Equity .... F

BUSINESS VITALITY — A

Business Competitiveness C
Entrepreneurial Energy C
Structural Diversity .... A

DEVELOPMENT CAPACITY — F

Human Resources .... F
Technology Resources .... D
Financial Resources .... F
Infrastructure & Amenity Resources .... F

Tax & Fiscal System — +

- **Economic Performance:** Mississippi improved a letter grade from last year, led by a jump in short-term employment growth and a decrease in unemployment. Nevertheless, earnings and job quality in the state are very poor and the state continues to have the worst poverty rate in the country.

- **Business Vitality:** With improving entrepreneurial energy, making the top twenty in new business job growth and growth in new companies, Mississippi's grade improved to an "A" this year. Structural diversity remains a plus.

- **Development Capacity:** Mississippi's development resources are the weakest in the nation. With the fourth worst high school graduation rate and the sixth worst college graduation rate, the state's human resources are the nation's weakest. Financial, infrastructure and amenity resources also receive failing marks.

Five Year Grade Trends

Key	
Economic Performance	————
Business Vitality	————
Development Capacity	- - - -

For more information on how grades and ranks are calculated, see the Methodology section.
For a detailed explanation of indexes, refer to the individual index section.

WHERE MISSISSIPPI RANKS – MEASURE BY MEASURE

		50th	40th	30th	20th	10th	1st

ECONOMIC PERFORMANCE INDEX MEASURES

Employment	Long-Term Employment Growth (24)
	Short-Term Employment Growth (6)
	Unemployment Rate (27)
	Unemployment Duration (22)
Earnings & Job Quality	Average Annual Pay (48)
	Average Annual Pay Growth (37)
	Health Coverage (48)
Equity	Poverty Rate (50)
	Income Distribution (45)
	Income Distribution Change (14)
	Rural/Urban Disparity (27)
Environmental, Social & Health Conditions	Air Quality (1)
	Superfund Dumpsites (2)
	Hazardous Waste Generation (43)
	Surface Water Discharge (1)
	Infant Mortality (48)
	Crime Rate (11)
	Teen Pregnancy (50)
	Heart Disease (49)
	Cancer Cases (38)
	Infectious Diseases (19)

BUSINESS VITALITY INDEX MEASURES

Competitiveness of Existing Business	Traded Sector Strength (35)
	Change in Traded Sector Strength (18)
	Business Closings (28)
	Manufacturing Capital Investment (16)
Entrepreneurial Energy	New Companies (34)
	Change in New Companies (20)
	New Business Job Growth (19)
Structural Diversity	Sectoral Diversity (11)
	Dynamic Diversity (5)

DEVELOPMENT CAPACITY INDEX MEASURES

Human Resources	High School Graduation (47)
	High School Education Attainment (49)
	College Education Attainment (45)
Technology Resources	Ph.D. Scientists & Engineers in Workforce (32)
	Science/Engineering Graduate Students (45)
	Patents Issued (50)
	University Research & Development (44)
	Federal Research & Development (30)
	SBIR Grants (39)
Financial Resources	Commercial Bank Deposits (37)
	Loans to Deposits (41)
	Loans to Equity (37)
	Commercial & Industrial Loans (40)
	Comm. & Ind. Loans to Total Loans (38)
	Venture Capital Investments (37)
	SBIC Financings (36)
Infrastructure & Amenity Resources	Highway Deficiency (46)
	Bridge Deficiency (40)
	Urban Mass Transit Availability (49)
	Energy Cost (24)
	Sewage Treatment Needs (19)
	Urban Housing Costs (16)
	Health Professional Shortage Areas (50)
	Tourism Spending (44)

TAX & FISCAL SYSTEM INDEX MEASURES

	Total Tax & Fiscal System Score (15)
	Fiscal Stability & Balanced Revenue (25)
	Tax Fairness (33)
	Fiscal Equalization (4)

		50th	40th	30th	20th	10th	1st

MISSOURI 1994 REPORT CARD

ECONOMIC PERFORMANCE	F
Employment .... D	
Earnings & Job Quality C	
Equity .... F	

BUSINESS VITALITY	B
Business Competitiveness .... F	
Entrepreneurial Energy .... B	
Structural Diversity .... A	

DEVELOPMENT CAPACITY	C
Human Resources C	
Technology Resources C	
Financial Resources C	
Infrastructure & Amenity Resources................. C	

Tax & Fiscal System	√

- **Economic Performance:** Missouri experienced the worst drop in performance of any state. With a slowing in long-term job growth and an increase in unemployment, job opportunities have worsened. Job quality is also the weakest in the region. Most troubling of all is a sharp drop in the rank for change in income distribution, leading to the nation's second worst score on measures of equity.

- **Business Vitality:** Fueled by a well diversified economy and the nation's third best new business job growth, Missouri's grade improved two letter grades from last year. However, the competitiveness of existing businesses remains weak.

- **Development Capacity:** As was the case with last year's Report Card, Missouri's development resources are average across the board. Highlights include low urban housing costs and strong bank deposits per capita. High bridge deficiency is a weaknesses.

Five Year Grade Trends

1990   1991   1992   1993   1994

Key

Economic Performance	————
Business Vitality	————
Development Capacity	- - - -

For more information on how grades and ranks are calculated, see the Methodology section.
For a detailed explanation of indexes, refer to the individual index section.

WHERE MISSOURI RANKS – MEASURE BY MEASURE

Scale: 50th 40th 30th 20th 10th 1st

ECONOMIC PERFORMANCE INDEX MEASURES

Employment
Long-Term Employment Growth (36)
Short-Term Employment Growth (48)
Unemployment Rate (28)
Unemployment Duration (29)

Earnings & Job Quality
Average Annual Pay (24)
Average Annual Pay Growth (41)
Health Coverage (28)

Equity
Poverty Rate (36)
Income Distribution (42)
Income Distribution Change (48)
Rural/Urban Disparity (39)

Environmental, Social & Health Conditions
Air Quality (24)
Superfund Dumpsites (22)
Hazardous Waste Generation (24)
Surface Water Discharge (36)
Infant Mortality (32)
Crime Rate (26)
Teen Pregnancy (32)
Heart Disease (31)
Cancer Cases (41)
Infectious Diseases (31)

BUSINESS VITALITY INDEX MEASURES

Competitiveness of Existing Business
Traded Sector Strength (36)
Change in Traded Sector Strength (49)
Business Closings (21)
Manufacturing Capital Investment (41)

Entrepreneurial Energy
New Companies (36)
Change in New Companies (26)
New Business Job Growth (3)

Structural Diversity
Sectoral Diversity (7)
Dynamic Diversity (16)

DEVELOPMENT CAPACITY INDEX MEASURES

Human Resources
High School Graduation (30)
High School Education Attainment (24)
College Education Attainment (25)

Technology Resources
Ph.D. Scientists & Engineers in Workforce (26)
Science/Engineering Graduate Students (35)
Patents Issued (27)
University Research & Development (30)
Federal Research & Development (24)
SBIR Grants (38)

Financial Resources
Commercial Bank Deposits (11)
Loans to Deposits (36)
Loans to Equity (31)
Commercial & Industrial Loans (15)
Comm. & Ind. Loans to Total Loans (18)
Venture Capital Investments (30)
SBIC Financings (39)

Infrastructure & Amenity Resources
Highway Deficiency (27)
Bridge Deficiency (47)
Urban Mass Transit Availability (21)
Energy Cost (27)
Sewage Treatment Needs (21)
Urban Housing Costs (2)
Health Professional Shortage Areas (33)
Tourism Spending (22)

TAX & FISCAL SYSTEM INDEX MEASURES

Total Tax & Fiscal System Score (27)
Fiscal Stability & Balanced Revenue (22)
Tax Fairness (31)
Fiscal Equalization (24)

Scale: 50th 40th 30th 20th 10th 1st

MONTANA 1994 REPORT CARD

ECONOMIC PERFORMANCE — D

Employment C
Earnings & Job Quality .... F
Equity .... B

BUSINESS VITALITY — B

Business Competitiveness C
Entrepreneurial Energy .... A
Structural Diversity C

DEVELOPMENT CAPACITY — B

Human Resources .... B
Technology Resources C
Financial Resources C
Infrastructure & Amenity Resources................... A

Tax & Fiscal System — √

- **Economic Performance:** Montana's grade dropped a letter this year as job quality, marked by a slowdown in pay growth and a decrease in health coverage, fell to a failing grade. Job opportunities remain modest, but are the second weakest in the region. Pluses include good income distribution and strong environmental quality.

- **Business Vitality:** Montana continues to benefit from a strong entrepreneurial climate. However, despite the nation's highest level of new manufacturing capital investments, a very weak traded sector weakens competitiveness.

- **Development Capacity:** Montana's grade improved again this year. With low energy costs, strong sewage treatment, and improved highways, infrastructure resources are now the state's highest ranking resource. Human resources continue to be a strength and financial and technology resources show modest improvement.

Five Year Grade Trends

| | 1990 | 1991 | 1992 | 1993 | 1994 |

Key
Economic Performance ———
Business Vitality ░░░░░░
Development Capacity – – –

For more information on how grades and ranks are calculated, see the Methodology section.
For a detailed explanation of indexes, refer to the individual index section.

WHERE MONTANA RANKS – MEASURE BY MEASURE

ECONOMIC PERFORMANCE INDEX MEASURES

Scale: 50th — 40th — 30th — 20th — 10th — 1st

Employment	Long-Term Employment Growth (38)
	Short-Term Employment Growth (29)
	Unemployment Rate (19)
	Unemployment Duration (20)
Earnings & Job Quality	Average Annual Pay (47)
	Average Annual Pay Growth (43)
	Health Coverage (37)
Equity	Poverty Rate (28)
	Income Distribution (17)
	Income Distribution Change (23)
	Rural/Urban Disparity (25)
Environmental, Social & Health Conditions	Air Quality (14)
	Superfund Dumpsites (43)
	Hazardous Waste Generation (6)
	Surface Water Discharge (6)
	Infant Mortality (11)
	Crime Rate (18)
	Teen Pregnancy (14)
	Heart Disease (6)
	Cancer Cases (24)
	Infectious Diseases (20)

BUSINESS VITALITY INDEX MEASURES

Competitiveness of Existing Business	Traded Sector Strength (49)
	Change in Traded Sector Strength (47)
	Business Closings (27)
	Manufacturing Capital Investment (1)
Entrepreneurial Energy	New Companies (9)
	Change in New Companies (3)
	New Business Job Growth (36)
Structural Diversity	Sectoral Diversity (37)
	Dynamic Diversity (12)

DEVELOPMENT CAPACITY INDEX MEASURES

Human Resources	High School Graduation (5)
	High School Education Attainment (10)
	College Education Attainment (25)
Technology Resources	Ph.D. Scientists & Engineers in Workforce (17)
	Science/Engineering Graduate Students (25)
	Patents Issued (34)
	University Research & Development (35)
	Federal Research & Development (42)
	SBIR Grants (36)
Financial Resources	Commercial Bank Deposits (35)
	Loans to Deposits (37)
	Loans to Equity (34)
	Commercial & Industrial Loans (31)
	Comm. & Ind. Loans to Total Loans (24)
	Venture Capital Investments (8)
	SBIC Financings (37)
Infrastructure & Amenity Resources	Highway Deficiency (24)
	Bridge Deficiency (10)
	Urban Mass Transit Availability (37)
	Energy Cost (3)
	Sewage Treatment Needs (4)
	Urban Housing Costs (1)
	Health Professional Shortage Areas (37)
	Tourism Spending (7)

TAX & FISCAL SYSTEM INDEX MEASURES

Total Tax & Fiscal System Score (16)
Fiscal Stability & Balanced Revenue (45)
Tax Fairness (6)
Fiscal Equalization (11)

Scale: 50th — 40th — 30th — 20th — 10th — 1st

NEBRASKA 1994 REPORT CARD

ECONOMIC PERFORMANCE	A

Employment	A
Earnings & Job Quality	C
Equity	A

BUSINESS VITALITY	D

Business Competitiveness	C
Entrepreneurial Energy	C
Structural Diversity	C

DEVELOPMENT CAPACITY	B

Human Resources	A
Technology Resources	D
Financial Resources	C
Infrastructure & Amenity Resources	A

Tax & Fiscal System	√

- **Economic Performance:** Bouncing back from the recession, Nebraska has the eighth best economic performance. Its unemployment rate was the nation's lowest and its short-term employment growth was strong. It also has the country's second best equity rating. Only average annual pay is poor though improving.

- **Business Vitality:** In contrast to its Economic Performance, Nebraska's Vitality ranks a poor 44th. Manufacturing capital investment, change in new companies, and structural diversity all rank in the bottom five. Yet, new business job growth was strong, complementing the state's strong employment showing.

- **Development Capacity**: Nebraska's strong capacity is due to excellent human resources and infrastructure. High school attainment ranks fifth, graduation third. Highway deficiency, energy cost, sewage needs and urban housing costs are in the top ten. Technology resources are weak.

Five Year Grade Trends

	1990	1991	1992	1993	1994
A					
B					
C					
D					
F					

Key

Economic Performance	———
Business Vitality	~~~~~
Development Capacity	- - -

For more information on how grades and ranks are calculated, see the Methodology section.
For a detailed explanation of indexes, refer to the individual index section.

WHERE NEBRASKA RANKS – MEASURE BY MEASURE

		50th	40th	30th	20th	10th	1st

ECONOMIC PERFORMANCE INDEX MEASURES

Employment
- Long-Term Employment Growth (34)
- Short-Term Employment Growth (18)
- Unemployment Rate (1)
- Unemployment Duration (6)

Earnings & Job Quality
- Average Annual Pay (45)
- Average Annual Pay Growth (26)
- Health Coverage (20)

Equity
- Poverty Rate (9)
- Income Distribution (3)
- Income Distribution Change (6)
- Rural/Urban Disparity (29)

Environmental, Social & Health Conditions
- Air Quality (1)
- Superfund Dumpsites (31)
- Hazardous Waste Generation (10)
- Surface Water Discharge (38)
- Infant Mortality (13)
- Crime Rate (14)
- Teen Pregnancy (7)
- Heart Disease (16)
- Cancer Cases (25)
- Infectious Diseases (6)

BUSINESS VITALITY INDEX MEASURES

Competitiveness of Existing Business
- Traded Sector Strength (22)
- Change in Traded Sector Strength (15)
- Business Closings (25)
- Manufacturing Capital Investment (47)

Entrepreneurial Energy
- New Companies (39)
- Change in New Companies (46)
- New Business Job Growth (5)

Structural Diversity
- Sectoral Diversity (46)
- Dynamic Diversity (13)

DEVELOPMENT CAPACITY INDEX MEASURES

Human Resources
- High School Graduation (3)
- High School Education Attainment (5)
- College Education Attainment (25)

Technology Resources
- Ph.D. Scientists & Engineers in Workforce (36)
- Science/Engineering Graduate Students (27)
- Patents Issued (42)
- University Research & Development (14)
- Federal Research & Development (43)
- SBIR Grants (30)

Financial Resources
- Commercial Bank Deposits (4)
- Loans to Deposits (34)
- Loans to Equity (30)
- Commercial & Industrial Loans (26)
- Comm. & Ind. Loans to Total Loans (41)
- Venture Capital Investments (31)
- SBIC Financings (41)

Infrastructure & Amenity Resources
- Highway Deficiency (10)
- Bridge Deficiency (35)
- Urban Mass Transit Availability (28)
- Energy Cost (10)
- Sewage Treatment Needs (9)
- Urban Housing Costs (9)
- Health Professional Shortage Areas (30)
- Tourism Spending (34)

TAX & FISCAL SYSTEM INDEX MEASURES
- Total Tax & Fiscal System Score (20)
- Fiscal Stability & Balanced Revenue (9)
- Tax Fairness (11)
- Fiscal Equalization (48)

		50th	40th	30th	20th	10th	1st

NEVADA 1994 REPORT CARD

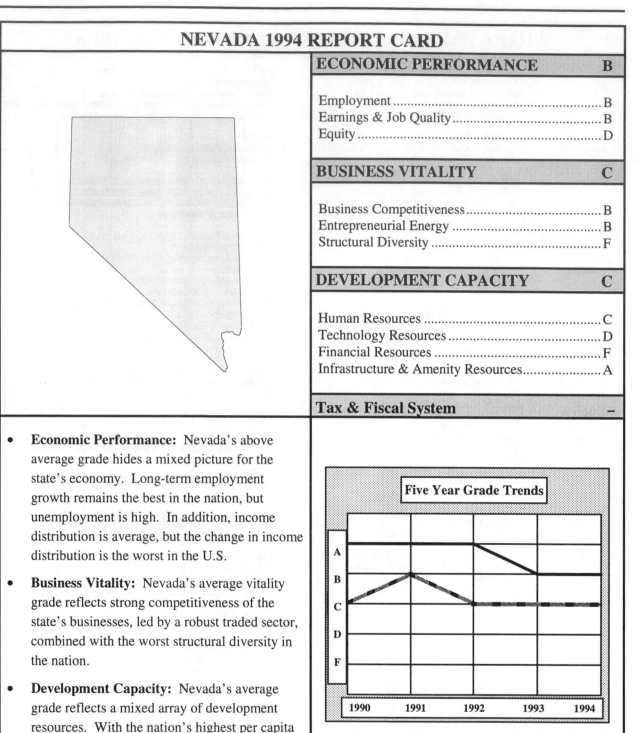

ECONOMIC PERFORMANCE	B
Employment	B
Earnings & Job Quality	B
Equity	D

BUSINESS VITALITY	C
Business Competitiveness	B
Entrepreneurial Energy	B
Structural Diversity	F

DEVELOPMENT CAPACITY	C
Human Resources	C
Technology Resources	D
Financial Resources	F
Infrastructure & Amenity Resources	A

Tax & Fiscal System	–

Five Year Grade Trends

1990   1991   1992   1993   1994

Key
Economic Performance ———
Business Vitality ~~~~~~
Development Capacity – – –

- **Economic Performance:** Nevada's above average grade hides a mixed picture for the state's economy. Long-term employment growth remains the best in the nation, but unemployment is high. In addition, income distribution is average, but the change in income distribution is the worst in the U.S.

- **Business Vitality:** Nevada's average vitality grade reflects strong competitiveness of the state's businesses, led by a robust traded sector, combined with the worst structural diversity in the nation.

- **Development Capacity:** Nevada's average grade reflects a mixed array of development resources. With the nation's highest per capita tourism receipts and strong bridges and sewers, Nevada's infrastructure and amenities resources are among the best in the nation. However, technology resources are below average and financial resources receive a failing grade.

For more information on how grades and ranks are calculated, see the Methodology section.
For a detailed explanation of indexes, refer to the individual index section.

WHERE NEVADA RANKS – MEASURE BY MEASURE

		50th 40th 30th 20th 10th 1st

ECONOMIC PERFORMANCE INDEX MEASURES

Employment
Long-Term Employment Growth (1)
Short-Term Employment Growth (8)
Unemployment Rate (36)
Unemployment Duration (27)

Earnings & Job Quality
Average Annual Pay (20)
Average Annual Pay Growth (2)
Health Coverage (33)

Equity
Poverty Rate (29)
Income Distribution (24)
Income Distribution Change (50)
Rural/Urban Disparity (15)

Environmental, Social & Health Conditions
Air Quality (22)
Superfund Dumpsites (1)
Hazardous Waste Generation (4)
Surface Water Discharge (50)
Infant Mortality (4)
Crime Rate (42)
Teen Pregnancy (40)
Heart Disease (44)
Cancer Cases (16)
Infectious Diseases (42)

BUSINESS VITALITY INDEX MEASURES

Competitiveness of Existing Business
Traded Sector Strength (8)
Change in Traded Sector Strength (1)
Business Closings (50)
Manufacturing Capital Investment (18)

Entrepreneurial Energy
New Companies (15)
Change in New Companies (10)
New Business Job Growth (41)

Structural Diversity
Sectoral Diversity (50)
Dynamic Diversity (44)

DEVELOPMENT CAPACITY INDEX MEASURES

Human Resources
High School Graduation (20)
High School Education Attainment (5)
College Education Attainment (39)

Technology Resources
Ph.D. Scientists & Engineers in Workforce (48)
Science/Engineering Graduate Students (48)
Patents Issued (35)
University Research & Development (36)
Federal Research & Development (9)
SBIR Grants (16)

Financial Resources
Commercial Bank Deposits (41)
Loans to Deposits (6)
Loans to Equity (48)
Commercial & Industrial Loans (49)
Comm. & Ind. Loans to Total Loans (49)
Venture Capital Investments (37)
SBIC Financings (22)

Infrastructure & Amenity Resources
Highway Deficiency (19)
Bridge Deficiency (3)
Urban Mass Transit Availability (26)
Energy Cost (16)
Sewage Treatment Needs (6)
Urban Housing Costs (40)
Health Professional Shortage Areas (21)
Tourism Spending (1)

TAX & FISCAL SYSTEM INDEX MEASURES

Total Tax & Fiscal System Score (46)
Fiscal Stability & Balanced Revenue (46)
Tax Fairness (44)
Fiscal Equalization (23)

50th 40th 30th 20th 10th 1st

NEW HAMPSHIRE 1994 REPORT CARD

ECONOMIC PERFORMANCE	A

Employment .... D
Earnings & Job Quality .... A
Equity .... A

BUSINESS VITALITY	D

Business Competitiveness .... D
Entrepreneurial Energy .... B
Structural Diversity .... D

DEVELOPMENT CAPACITY	C

Human Resources .... B
Technology Resources .... B
Financial Resources .... D
Infrastructure & Amenity Resources .... F

Tax & Fiscal System	–

- **Economic Performance:** Equity and earnings and job quality are good, but employment is not. Short- and long-term employment growth are near the median, but unemployment duration is 42nd and change in income distribution is 49th, raising questions if the recession closed off opportunities for some.

- **Business Vitality:** Diversity is low and existing businesses are not very competitive as closings are high and manufacturing investment the lowest in the country. The bright spot is the high number of new companies, but this may reflect a lack of options because new business job growth is 50th and unemployment duration is long.

- **Development Capacity:** The state's strong human and technology resources (including 4th highest college attainment and 4th highest of SBIR grants) position it well for future growth in high-value added sectors. Weak financial activity and poor infrastructure are hurdles.

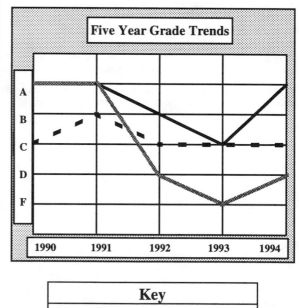

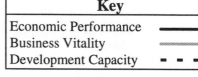

Key	
Economic Performance	——
Business Vitality	~~~~~
Development Capacity	- - -

For more information on how grades and ranks are calculated, see the Methodology section.
For a detailed explanation of indexes, refer to the individual index section.

The Corporation for Enterprise Development

WHERE NEW HAMPSHIRE RANKS – MEASURE BY MEASURE

		50th	40th	30th	20th	10th	1st

ECONOMIC PERFORMANCE INDEX MEASURES

Employment	Long-Term Employment Growth (26)
	Short-Term Employment Growth (26)
	Unemployment Rate (30)
	Unemployment Duration (42)

Earnings & Job Quality	Average Annual Pay (18)
	Average Annual Pay Growth (13)
	Health Coverage (16)

Equity	Poverty Rate (2)
	Income Distribution (12)
	Income Distribution Change (49)
	Rural/Urban Disparity (4)

Environmental, Social & Health Conditions	Air Quality (23)
	Superfund Dumpsites (49)
	Hazardous Waste Generation (8)
	Surface Water Discharge (14)
	Infant Mortality (1)
	Crime Rate (4)
	Teen Pregnancy (1)
	Heart Disease (26)
	Cancer Cases (25)
	Infectious Diseases (4)

BUSINESS VITALITY INDEX MEASURES

Competitiveness of Existing Business	Traded Sector Strength (13)
	Change in Traded Sector Strength (33)
	Business Closings (37)
	Manufacturing Capital Investment (50)

Entrepreneurial Energy	New Companies (8)
	Change in New Companies (2)
	New Business Job Growth (50)

| *Structural Diversity* | Sectoral Diversity (34) |
| | Dynamic Diversity (34) |

DEVELOPMENT CAPACITY INDEX MEASURES

Human Resources	High School Graduation (22)
	High School Education Attainment (16)
	College Education Attainment (4)

Technology Resources	Ph.D. Scientists & Engineers in Workforce (21)
	Science/Engineering Graduate Students (44)
	Patents Issued (6)
	University Research & Development (17)
	Federal Research & Development (17)
	SBIR Grants (4)

Financial Resources	Commercial Bank Deposits (50)
	Loans to Deposits (17)
	Loans to Equity (16)
	Commercial & Industrial Loans (50)
	Comm. & Ind. Loans to Total Loans (48)
	Venture Capital Investments (3)
	SBIC Financings (42)

Infrastructure & Amenity Resources	Highway Deficiency (50)
	Bridge Deficiency (38)
	Urban Mass Transit Availability (42)
	Energy Cost (49)
	Sewage Treatment Needs (46)
	Urban Housing Costs (21)
	Health Professional Shortage Areas (3)
	Tourism Spending (36)

TAX & FISCAL SYSTEM INDEX MEASURES

	Total Tax & Fiscal System Score (49)
	Fiscal Stability & Balanced Revenue (49)
	Tax Fairness (25)
	Fiscal Equalization (50)

		50th	40th	30th	20th	10th	1st

NEW JERSEY 1994 REPORT CARD

ECONOMIC PERFORMANCE	C
Employment	F
Earnings & Job Quality	A
Equity	C

BUSINESS VITALITY	A
Business Competitiveness	A
Entrepreneurial Energy	A
Structural Diversity	C

DEVELOPMENT CAPACITY	A
Human Resources	A
Technology Resources	B
Financial Resources	A
Infrastructure & Amenity Resources	D

Tax & Fiscal System	–

- **Economic Performance:** New Jersey's average economic performance hides great differences in employment and job quality. With high unemployment and slow job growth, New Jersey has the third worst employment market in the country. However, the state also boasts the nation's second best job quality, with top pay and strong health coverage.

- **Business Vitality:** New Jersey's grade improved two letters from last year and now shows the third best score in the country. This rapid rise was fueled by continued strength in the competitiveness of the state's firms as well as a turnaround from "F" to "A" on entrepreneurial energy.

- **Development Capacity:** Led by improved human resources and continued strength in its technology and financial resources, New Jersey's grade improved a letter from last year. Infrastructure and amenity resources remain weak.

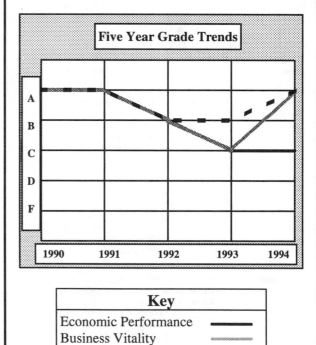

Five Year Grade Trends

	1990	1991	1992	1993	1994

Key

Economic Performance	———
Business Vitality	━━━
Development Capacity	– – –

For more information on how grades and ranks are calculated, see the Methodology section.
For a detailed explanation of indexes, refer to the individual index section.

The Corporation for Enterprise Development

WHERE NEW JERSEY RANKS – MEASURE BY MEASURE

| | | 50th | 40th | 30th | 20th | 10th | 1st |

ECONOMIC PERFORMANCE INDEX MEASURES

Employment
Long-Term Employment Growth (44)
Short-Term Employment Growth (41)
Unemployment Rate (38)
Unemployment Duration (46)

Earnings & Job Quality
Average Annual Pay (3)
Average Annual Pay Growth (3)
Health Coverage (12)

Equity
Poverty Rate (6)
Income Distribution (30)
Income Distribution Change (43)
Rural/Urban Disparity (24)

Environmental, Social & Health Conditions
Air Quality (49)
Superfund Dumpsites (47)
Hazardous Waste Generation (45)
Surface Water Discharge (26)
Infant Mortality (20)
Crime Rate (25)
Teen Pregnancy (7)
Heart Disease (30)
Cancer Cases (44)
Infectious Diseases (38)

BUSINESS VITALITY INDEX MEASURES

Competitiveness of Existing Business
Traded Sector Strength (2)
Change in Traded Sector Strength (6)
Business Closings (23)
Manufacturing Capital Investment (33)

Entrepreneurial Energy
New Companies (22)
Change in New Companies (11)
New Business Job Growth (23)

Structural Diversity
Sectoral Diversity (29)
Dynamic Diversity (29)

DEVELOPMENT CAPACITY INDEX MEASURES

Human Resources
High School Graduation (8)
High School Education Attainment (19)
College Education Attainment (4)

Technology Resources
Ph.D. Scientists & Engineers in Workforce (8)
Science/Engineering Graduate Students (32)
Patents Issued (4)
University Research & Development (41)
Federal Research & Development (13)
SBIR Grants (14)

Financial Resources
Commercial Bank Deposits (9)
Loans to Deposits (37)
Loans to Equity (11)
Commercial & Industrial Loans (17)
Comm. & Ind. Loans to Total Loans (23)
Venture Capital Investments (21)
SBIC Financings (10)

Infrastructure & Amenity Resources
Highway Deficiency (28)
Bridge Deficiency (45)
Urban Mass Transit Availability (2)
Energy Cost (44)
Sewage Treatment Needs (43)
Urban Housing Costs (42)
Health Professional Shortage Areas (8)
Tourism Spending (19)

TAX & FISCAL SYSTEM INDEX MEASURES

Total Tax & Fiscal System Score (37)
Fiscal Stability & Balanced Revenue (30)
Tax Fairness (27)
Fiscal Equalization (38)

| | | 50th | 40th | 30th | 20th | 10th | 1st |

NEW MEXICO 1994 REPORT CARD

ECONOMIC PERFORMANCE	D
Employment	C
Earnings & Job Quality	F
Equity	C

BUSINESS VITALITY	B
Business Competitiveness	F
Entrepreneurial Energy	A
Structural Diversity	A

DEVELOPMENT CAPACITY	C
Human Resources	C
Technology Resources	A
Financial Resources	F
Infrastructure & Amenity Resources	C

Tax & Fiscal System	+

- **Economic Performance:** New Mexico does a good job of creating employment opportunities, ranking 11th nationally in long-term employment growth rate. Yet, job quality is poor and, with high poverty and unemployment rates, the benefits of growth are spread unevenly.

- **Business Vitality:** Although down a grade from last year, New Mexico's vitality remains strong, led by the growth of new company formations and dynamic diversity. However, the competitiveness of existing businesses is poor.

- **Development Capacity:** New Mexico's average grade reflects mixed investment in development resources. The state ranks second in the nation in technology resources. However, the state's human and infrastructure resources receive only average grades, while the state's financial resources rank last.

Five Year Grade Trends

Key	
Economic Performance	————
Business Vitality	▓▓▓▓▓
Development Capacity	– – – –

For more information on how grades and ranks are calculated, see the Methodology section.
For a detailed explanation of indexes, refer to the individual index section.

WHERE NEW MEXICO RANKS – MEASURE BY MEASURE

ECONOMIC PERFORMANCE INDEX MEASURES

| | | 50th | 40th | 30th | 20th | 10th | 1st |

Employment
Long-Term Employment Growth (11)
Short-Term Employment Growth (32)
Unemployment Rate (41)
Unemployment Duration (16)

Earnings &
Job Quality
Average Annual Pay (42)
Average Annual Pay Growth (45)
Health Coverage (46)

Equity
Poverty Rate (47)
Income Distribution (44)
Income Distribution Change (19)
Rural/Urban Disparity (3)

Environmental,
Social &
Health
Conditions
Air Quality (16)
Superfund Dumpsites (35)
Hazardous Waste Generation (20)
Surface Water Discharge (22)
Infant Mortality (17)
Crime Rate (45)
Teen Pregnancy (47)
Heart Disease (2)
Cancer Cases (5)
Infectious Diseases (48)

BUSINESS VITALITY INDEX MEASURES

Competitiveness
of Existing
Business
Traded Sector Strength (48)
Change in Traded Sector Strength (42)
Business Closings (26)
Manufacturing Capital Investment (28)

Entrepreneurial
Energy
New Companies (14)
Change in New Companies (5)
New Business Job Growth (28)

Structural
Diversity
Sectoral Diversity (19)
Dynamic Diversity (3)

DEVELOPMENT CAPACITY INDEX MEASURES

Human
Resources
High School Graduation (38)
High School Education Attainment (24)
College Education Attainment (19)

Technology
Resources
Ph.D. Scientists & Engineers in Workforce (2)
Science/Engineering Graduate Students (7)
Patents Issued (26)
University Research & Development (3)
Federal Research & Development (1)
SBIR Grants (2)

Financial
Resources
Commercial Bank Deposits (44)
Loans to Deposits (47)
Loans to Equity (34)
Commercial & Industrial Loans (46)
Comm. & Ind. Loans to Total Loans (39)
Venture Capital Investments (37)
SBIC Financings (44)

Infrastructure
& Amenity
Resources
Highway Deficiency (38)
Bridge Deficiency (2)
Urban Mass Transit Availability (32)
Energy Cost (35)
Sewage Treatment Needs (3)
Urban Housing Costs (46)
Health Professional Shortage Areas (47)
Tourism Spending (14)

TAX & FISCAL SYSTEM INDEX MEASURES

Total Tax & Fiscal System Score (4)
Fiscal Stability & Balanced Revenue (14)
Tax Fairness (35)
Fiscal Equalization (1)

| | | 50th | 40th | 30th | 20th | 10th | 1st |

NEW YORK 1994 REPORT CARD

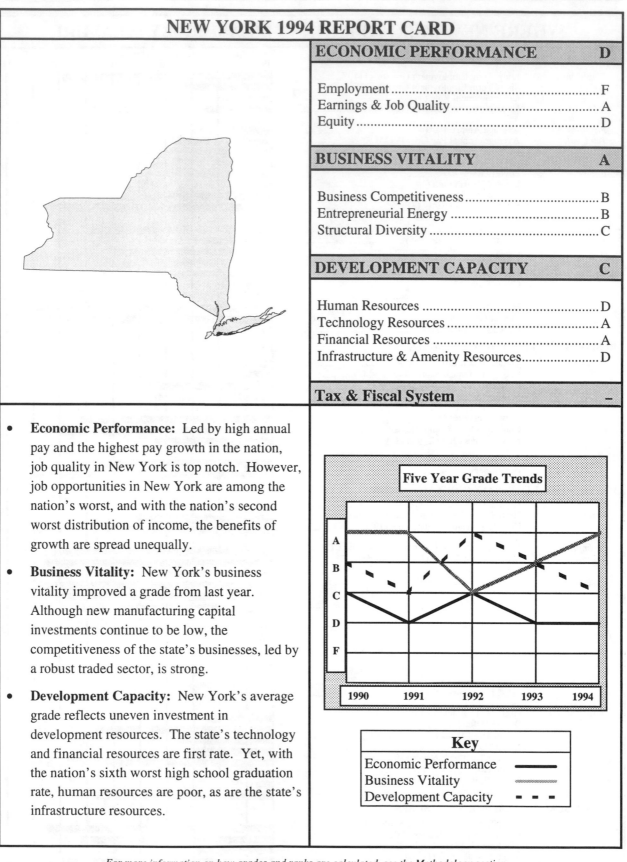

ECONOMIC PERFORMANCE	D
Employment	F
Earnings & Job Quality	A
Equity	D

BUSINESS VITALITY	A
Business Competitiveness	B
Entrepreneurial Energy	B
Structural Diversity	C

DEVELOPMENT CAPACITY	C
Human Resources	D
Technology Resources	A
Financial Resources	A
Infrastructure & Amenity Resources	D

Tax & Fiscal System	–

- **Economic Performance:** Led by high annual pay and the highest pay growth in the nation, job quality in New York is top notch. However, job opportunities in New York are among the nation's worst, and with the nation's second worst distribution of income, the benefits of growth are spread unequally.

- **Business Vitality:** New York's business vitality improved a grade from last year. Although new manufacturing capital investments continue to be low, the competitiveness of the state's businesses, led by a robust traded sector, is strong.

- **Development Capacity:** New York's average grade reflects uneven investment in development resources. The state's technology and financial resources are first rate. Yet, with the nation's sixth worst high school graduation rate, human resources are poor, as are the state's infrastructure resources.

Five Year Grade Trends

	1990	1991	1992	1993	1994

Key

Economic Performance	——
Business Vitality	▨▨▨
Development Capacity	– – –

For more information on how grades and ranks are calculated, see the Methodology section.
For a detailed explanation of indexes, refer to the individual index section.

WHERE NEW YORK RANKS – MEASURE BY MEASURE

ECONOMIC PERFORMANCE INDEX MEASURES

| | | 50th | 40th | 30th | 20th | 10th | 1st |

Employment
- Long-Term Employment Growth (43)
- Short-Term Employment Growth (34)
- Unemployment Rate (46)
- Unemployment Duration (45)

Earnings & Job Quality
- Average Annual Pay (2)
- Average Annual Pay Growth (1)
- Health Coverage (31)

Equity
- Poverty Rate (33)
- Income Distribution (49)
- Income Distribution Change (29)
- Rural/Urban Disparity (7)

Environmental, Social & Health Conditions
- Air Quality (48)
- Superfund Dumpsites (23)
- Hazardous Waste Generation (18)
- Surface Water Discharge (29)
- Infant Mortality (30)
- Crime Rate (37)
- Teen Pregnancy (13)
- Heart Disease (46)
- Cancer Cases (33)
- Infectious Diseases (50)

BUSINESS VITALITY INDEX MEASURES

Competitiveness of Existing Business
- Traded Sector Strength (6)
- Change in Traded Sector Strength (3)
- Business Closings (24)
- Manufacturing Capital Investment (42)

Entrepreneurial Energy
- New Companies (22)
- Change in New Companies (16)
- New Business Job Growth (26)

Structural Diversity
- Sectoral Diversity (26)
- Dynamic Diversity (30)

DEVELOPMENT CAPACITY INDEX MEASURES

Human Resources
- High School Graduation (45)
- High School Education Attainment (35)
- College Education Attainment (14)

Technology Resources
- Ph.D. Scientists & Engineers in Workforce (9)
- Science/Engineering Graduate Students (6)
- Patents Issued (10)
- University Research & Development (13)
- Federal Research & Development (18)
- SBIR Grants (18)

Financial Resources
- Commercial Bank Deposits (3)
- Loans to Deposits (10)
- Loans to Equity (49)
- Commercial & Industrial Loans (1)
- Comm. & Ind. Loans to Total Loans (6)
- Venture Capital Investments (29)
- SBIC Financings (16)

Infrastructure & Amenity Resources
- Highway Deficiency (4)
- Bridge Deficiency (50)
- Urban Mass Transit Availability (1)
- Energy Cost (48)
- Sewage Treatment Needs (48)
- Urban Housing Costs (41)
- Health Professional Shortage Areas (36)
- Tourism Spending (29)

TAX & FISCAL SYSTEM INDEX MEASURES

- Total Tax & Fiscal System Score (41)
- Fiscal Stability & Balanced Revenue (29)
- Tax Fairness (21)
- Fiscal Equalization (49)

| | | 50th | 40th | 30th | 20th | 10th | 1st |

NORTH CAROLINA 1994 REPORT CARD

ECONOMIC PERFORMANCE	C
Employment	B
Earnings & Job Quality	C
Equity	C

BUSINESS VITALITY	C
Business Competitiveness	C
Entrepreneurial Energy	C
Structural Diversity	B

DEVELOPMENT CAPACITY	D
Human Resources	D
Technology Resources	C
Financial Resources	A
Infrastructure & Amenity Resources	D

Tax & Fiscal System	+

- **Economic Performance:** Due to a slight worsening in measures of equity, North Carolina's grade dropped one letter from last year. Nevertheless, the state benefits from strong long-term employment growth, the nation's 8th lowest unemployment rate, and the third best job quality ranking in the South.

- **Business Vitality:** Although North Carolina has a strong traded sector and shows good structural diversity, the state is hampered by low new manufacturing capital investment and the nation's second worst rate of business closings.

- **Development Capacity:** North Carolina's financial resources are fifth best in the nation and the best in the South. However, continued low levels of high school graduation and college attainment, as well as poor infrastructure resources, translate into a below average grade.

Five Year Grade Trends

Key	
Economic Performance	———
Business Vitality	▨▨▨▨
Development Capacity	- - -

For more information on how grades and ranks are calculated, see the Methodology section.
For a detailed explanation of indexes, refer to the individual index section.

WHERE NORTH CAROLINA RANKS – MEASURE BY MEASURE

ECONOMIC PERFORMANCE INDEX MEASURES

Employment
Long-Term Employment Growth (18)
Short-Term Employment Growth (31)
Unemployment Rate (8)
Unemployment Duration (18)

Earnings & Job Quality
Average Annual Pay (33)
Average Annual Pay Growth (16)
Health Coverage (29)

Equity
Poverty Rate (37)
Income Distribution (29)
Income Distribution Change (25)
Rural/Urban Disparity (21)

Environmental, Social & Health Conditions
Air Quality (25)
Superfund Dumpsites (11)
Hazardous Waste Generation (14)
Surface Water Discharge (16)
Infant Mortality (46)
Crime Rate (35)
Teen Pregnancy (36)
Heart Disease (33)
Cancer Cases (27)
Infectious Diseases (27)

BUSINESS VITALITY INDEX MEASURES

Competitiveness of Existing Business
Traded Sector Strength (16)
Change in Traded Sector Strength (11)
Business Closings (49)
Manufacturing Capital Investment (44)

Entrepreneurial Energy
New Companies (26)
Change in New Companies (36)
New Business Job Growth (16)

Structural Diversity
Sectoral Diversity (21)
Dynamic Diversity (19)

DEVELOPMENT CAPACITY INDEX MEASURES

Human Resources
High School Graduation (39)
High School Education Attainment (44)
College Education Attainment (36)

Technology Resources
Ph.D. Scientists & Engineers in Workforce (28)
Science/Engineering Graduate Students (33)
Patents Issued (32)
University Research & Development (15)
Federal Research & Development (27)
SBIR Grants (29)

Financial Resources
Commercial Bank Deposits (26)
Loans to Deposits (5)
Loans to Equity (6)
Commercial & Industrial Loans (9)
Comm. & Ind. Loans to Total Loans (9)
Venture Capital Investments (27)
SBIC Financings (22)

Infrastructure & Amenity Resources
Highway Deficiency (47)
Bridge Deficiency (36)
Urban Mass Transit Availability (39)
Energy Cost (31)
Sewage Treatment Needs (42)
Urban Housing Costs (23)
Health Professional Shortage Areas (35)
Tourism Spending (23)

TAX & FISCAL SYSTEM INDEX MEASURES

Total Tax & Fiscal System Score (12)
Fiscal Stability & Balanced Revenue (3)
Tax Fairness (36)
Fiscal Equalization (15)

Scale: 50th — 40th — 30th — 20th — 10th — 1st

NORTH DAKOTA 1994 REPORT CARD

ECONOMIC PERFORMANCE	D
Employment C	
Earnings & Job Quality .... D	
Equity .... B	

BUSINESS VITALITY	B
Business Competitiveness .... A	
Entrepreneurial Energy .... D	
Structural Diversity C	

DEVELOPMENT CAPACITY	C
Human Resources .... B	
Technology Resources C	
Financial Resources .... D	
Infrastructure & Amenity Resources .... B	

Tax & Fiscal System	+

- **Economic Performance:** North Dakota's economy is still performing poorly, but there are signs that this is changing. While long-term employment growth is very poor, short-term employment growth is above the median; average annual pay is second worst in the country, but is improving; and income distribution is good.

- **Business Vitality:** North Dakota's existing companies are its strength; they have high manufacturing capital investment and few are closing. The state's weakness is low entrepreneurship, especially few new companies and low new business job growth.

- **Development Capacity:** North Dakota has the baseline human resources and physical infrastructure it needs, including the second highest high school graduation, second fewest deficient highways and few sewage needs. But its financial resources are lacking, with few loans and little SBIC financing.

Five Year Grade Trends

Key
Economic Performance ———
Business Vitality ═══
Development Capacity – – –

For more information on how grades and ranks are calculated, see the Methodology section.
For a detailed explanation of indexes, refer to the individual index section.

WHERE NORTH DAKOTA RANKS – MEASURE BY MEASURE

		50th	40th	30th	20th	10th	1st

ECONOMIC PERFORMANCE INDEX MEASURES

Employment
Long-Term Employment Growth (49)
Short-Term Employment Growth (21)
Unemployment Rate (6)
Unemployment Duration (25)

Earnings & Job Quality
Average Annual Pay (49)
Average Annual Pay Growth (37)
Health Coverage (38)

Equity
Poverty Rate (22)
Income Distribution (13)
Income Distribution Change (11)
Rural/Urban Disparity (47)

Environmental, Social & Health Conditions
Air Quality (1)
Superfund Dumpsites (9)
Hazardous Waste Generation (38)
Surface Water Discharge (12)
Infant Mortality (6)
Crime Rate (2)
Teen Pregnancy (2)
Heart Disease (12)
Cancer Cases (34)
Infectious Diseases (1)

BUSINESS VITALITY INDEX MEASURES

Competitiveness of Existing Business
Traded Sector Strength (44)
Change in Traded Sector Strength (2)
Business Closings (4)
Manufacturing Capital Investment (7)

Entrepreneurial Energy
New Companies (43)
Change in New Companies (15)
New Business Job Growth (49)

Structural Diversity
Sectoral Diversity (47)
Dynamic Diversity (2)

DEVELOPMENT CAPACITY INDEX MEASURES

Human Resources
High School Graduation (2)
High School Education Attainment (32)
College Education Attainment (25)

Technology Resources
Ph.D. Scientists & Engineers in Workforce (10)
Science/Engineering Graduate Students (24)
Patents Issued (39)
University Research & Development (11)
Federal Research & Development (37)
SBIR Grants (40)

Financial Resources
Commercial Bank Deposits (10)
Loans to Deposits (42)
Loans to Equity (42)
Commercial & Industrial Loans (27)
Comm. & Ind. Loans to Total Loans (31)
Venture Capital Investments (37)
SBIC Financings (44)

Infrastructure & Amenity Resources
Highway Deficiency (2)
Bridge Deficiency (26)
Urban Mass Transit Availability (44)
Energy Cost (18)
Sewage Treatment Needs (2)
Urban Housing Costs (26)
Health Professional Shortage Areas (46)
Tourism Spending (15)

TAX & FISCAL SYSTEM INDEX MEASURES

Total Tax & Fiscal System Score (9)
Fiscal Stability & Balanced Revenue (33)
Tax Fairness (9)
Fiscal Equalization (19)

		50th	40th	30th	20th	10th	1st

OHIO 1994 REPORT CARD

ECONOMIC PERFORMANCE	C
Employment	D
Earnings & Job Quality	A
Equity	C

BUSINESS VITALITY	C
Business Competitiveness	B
Entrepreneurial Energy	F
Structural Diversity	B

DEVELOPMENT CAPACITY	B
Human Resources	C
Technology Resources	B
Financial Resources	B
Infrastructure & Amenity Resources	C

Tax & Fiscal System	√

- **Economic Performance:** Jobs in Ohio are good, there just are not enough of them. While existing jobs provide good health coverage and annual pay, Ohio's short- and long-term employment growth are low and its unemployment is fairly high.

- **Business Vitality:** Ohio's strong base but lack of dynamism is reflected in its business sector. The state has the second fewest business closings, a strong traded sector and a sectorally diverse economy. But, entrepreneurship is among the lowest in the nation, with the worst rate of new companies last year.

- **Development Capacity:** The state's resource strengths are in technology and finances. In particular, it has many science and engineering graduate students, patents and federal and SBIR grants to leverage. The heavy loan activity this past year can hopefully be used to encourage the poor local entrepreneurship.

Five Year Grade Trends

| | 1990 | 1991 | 1992 | 1993 | 1994 |

Key

Economic Performance ———
Business Vitality
Development Capacity – – –

For more information on how grades and ranks are calculated, see the Methodology section.
For a detailed explanation of indexes, refer to the individual index section.

WHERE OHIO RANKS – MEASURE BY MEASURE

| | | 50th | 40th | 30th | 20th | 10th | 1st |

ECONOMIC PERFORMANCE INDEX MEASURES

Employment
Long-Term Employment Growth (33)
Short-Term Employment Growth (37)
Unemployment Rate (29)
Unemployment Duration (35)

Earnings & Job Quality
Average Annual Pay (19)
Average Annual Pay Growth (19)
Health Coverage (10)

Equity
Poverty Rate (24)
Income Distribution (25)
Income Distribution Change (24)
Rural/Urban Disparity (34)

Environmental, Social & Health Conditions
Air Quality (37)
Superfund Dumpsites (16)
Hazardous Waste Generation (28)
Surface Water Discharge (47)
Infant Mortality (20)
Crime Rate (19)
Teen Pregnancy (30)
Heart Disease (40)
Cancer Cases (32)
Infectious Diseases (7)

BUSINESS VITALITY INDEX MEASURES

Competitiveness of Existing Business
Traded Sector Strength (11)
Change in Traded Sector Strength (39)
Business Closings (2)
Manufacturing Capital Investment (24)

Entrepreneurial Energy
New Companies (50)
Change in New Companies (40)
New Business Job Growth (32)

Structural Diversity
Sectoral Diversity (16)
Dynamic Diversity (27)

DEVELOPMENT CAPACITY INDEX MEASURES

Human Resources
High School Graduation (32)
High School Education Attainment (24)
College Education Attainment (32)

Technology Resources
Ph.D. Scientists & Engineers in Workforce (23)
Science/Engineering Graduate Students (10)
Patents Issued (12)
University Research & Development (40)
Federal Research & Development (20)
SBIR Grants (19)

Financial Resources
Commercial Bank Deposits (34)
Loans to Deposits (6)
Loans to Equity (5)
Commercial & Industrial Loans (14)
Comm. & Ind. Loans to Total Loans (22)
Venture Capital Investments (28)
SBIC Financings (21)

Infrastructure & Amenity Resources
Highway Deficiency (20)
Bridge Deficiency (25)
Urban Mass Transit Availability (16)
Energy Cost (23)
Sewage Treatment Needs (37)
Urban Housing Costs (12)
Health Professional Shortage Areas (18)
Tourism Spending (48)

TAX & FISCAL SYSTEM INDEX MEASURES

Total Tax & Fiscal System Score (18)
Fiscal Stability & Balanced Revenue (6)
Tax Fairness (30)
Fiscal Equalization (27)

| | | 50th | 40th | 30th | 20th | 10th | 1st |

OKLAHOMA 1994 REPORT CARD

ECONOMIC PERFORMANCE — D

Employment .... D
Earnings & Job Quality .... F
Equity C

BUSINESS VITALITY — F

Business Competitiveness .... D
Entrepreneurial Energy .... D
Structural Diversity C

DEVELOPMENT CAPACITY — D

Human Resources C
Technology Resources .... D
Financial Resources .... D
Infrastructure & Amenity Resources C

Tax & Fiscal System — √

- **Economic Performance:** Oklahoma's poor grade reflects weak employment opportunity, marked by the nation's third worst long-term job growth, combined with the nation's worst score for earnings and job quality. However, a strong rate of change in income distribution helped the state improve from last year's F.

- **Business Vitality:** One of the worst five states in terms of vitality, Oklahoma scores especially low on competitiveness, with a weak traded sector and low new manufacturing capital invesment, as well as poor entrepreneurial energy.

- **Development Capacity:** Oklahoma's technology and financial resources are weak, marked by low federal R&D spending and the nation's second lowest ratio of loans to deposits. Yet, though rated only average on human resources, the state benefits from above median college attainment and high school graduation rates.

Five Year Grade Trends

	1990	1991	1992	1993	1994
A					
B					
C					
D					
F					

Key

Economic Performance ———
Business Vitality ▓▓▓▓
Development Capacity - - -

For more information on how grades and ranks are calculated, see the Methodology section.
For a detailed explanation of indexes, refer to the individual index section.

WHERE OKLAHOMA RANKS – MEASURE BY MEASURE

		50th	40th	30th	20th	10th	1st

ECONOMIC PERFORMANCE INDEX MEASURES

Employment
Long-Term Employment Growth (48)
Short-Term Employment Growth (43)
Unemployment Rate (19)
Unemployment Duration (28)

Earnings & Job Quality
Average Annual Pay (39)
Average Annual Pay Growth (48)
Health Coverage (49)

Equity
Poverty Rate (44)
Income Distribution (40)
Income Distribution Change (11)
Rural/Urban Disparity (5)

Environmental, Social & Health Conditions
Air Quality (1)
Superfund Dumpsites (15)
Hazardous Waste Generation (32)
Surface Water Discharge (25)
Infant Mortality (34)
Crime Rate (30)
Teen Pregnancy (37)
Heart Disease (45)
Cancer Cases (30)
Infectious Diseases (24)

BUSINESS VITALITY INDEX MEASURES

Competitiveness of Existing Business
Traded Sector Strength (42)
Change in Traded Sector Strength (41)
Business Closings (15)
Manufacturing Capital Investment (33)

Entrepreneurial Energy
New Companies (25)
Change in New Companies (42)
New Business Job Growth (31)

Structural Diversity
Sectoral Diversity (27)
Dynamic Diversity (25)

DEVELOPMENT CAPACITY INDEX MEASURES

Human Resources
High School Graduation (24)
High School Education Attainment (35)
College Education Attainment (23)

Technology Resources
Ph.D. Scientists & Engineers in Workforce (32)
Science/Engineering Graduate Students (23)
Patents Issued (23)
University Research & Development (37)
Federal Research & Development (45)
SBIR Grants (34)

Financial Resources
Commercial Bank Deposits (29)
Loans to Deposits (49)
Loans to Equity (46)
Commercial & Industrial Loans (33)
Comm. & Ind. Loans to Total Loans (17)
Venture Capital Investments (36)
SBIC Financings (18)

Infrastructure & Amenity Resources
Highway Deficiency (30)
Bridge Deficiency (42)
Urban Mass Transit Availability (38)
Energy Cost (17)
Sewage Treatment Needs (8)
Urban Housing Costs (11)
Health Professional Shortage Areas (28)
Tourism Spending (25)

TAX & FISCAL SYSTEM INDEX MEASURES

Total Tax & Fiscal System Score (19)
Fiscal Stability & Balanced Revenue (26)
Tax Fairness (34)
Fiscal Equalization (14)

		50th	40th	30th	20th	10th	1st

OREGON 1994 REPORT CARD

ECONOMIC PERFORMANCE	B
Employment	B
Earnings & Job Quality	B
Equity	C

BUSINESS VITALITY	D
Business Competitiveness	D
Entrepreneurial Energy	B
Structural Diversity	D

DEVELOPMENT CAPACITY	A
Human Resources	C
Technology Resources	C
Financial Resources	A
Infrastructure & Amenity Resources	B

Tax & Fiscal System	–

- **Economic Performance:** With employment growth that is among the nation's best, as well as good pay and strong pay growth, Oregon's economy provides both good job quality and job opportunity. Due in part to above average population growth, however, unemployment continues to be a problem.

- **Business Vitality:** Despite healthy entrepreneurial energy, led by new business job growth, the state's business vitality is poor. Continued weakness in the traded sector, as well as poor structural diversity, are a problem.

- **Development Capacity:** Oregon's development resources receive an excellent grade this year. Highlights include first rate financial resources, including the nation's highest rate of SBIC financings, as well as good infrastructure and amenity resources.

Five Year Grade Trends

Key	
Economic Performance	———
Business Vitality	～～～
Development Capacity	- - -

For more information on how grades and ranks are calculated, see the Methodology section.
For a detailed explanation of indexes, refer to the individual index section.

WHERE OREGON RANKS – MEASURE BY MEASURE

ECONOMIC PERFORMANCE INDEX MEASURES

Employment	Long-Term Employment Growth (7)
	Short-Term Employment Growth (10)
	Unemployment Rate (36)
	Unemployment Duration (17)
Earnings & Job Quality	Average Annual Pay (25)
	Average Annual Pay Growth (19)
	Health Coverage (12)
Equity	Poverty Rate (17)
	Income Distribution (18)
	Income Distribution Change (37)
	Rural/Urban Disparity (34)
Environmental, Social & Health Conditions	Air Quality (21)
	Superfund Dumpsites (20)
	Hazardous Waste Generation (12)
	Surface Water Discharge (8)
	Infant Mortality (13)
	Crime Rate (36)
	Teen Pregnancy (23)
	Heart Disease (9)
	Cancer Cases (31)
	Infectious Diseases (46)

BUSINESS VITALITY INDEX MEASURES

Competitiveness of Existing Business	Traded Sector Strength (38)
	Change in Traded Sector Strength (37)
	Business Closings (39)
	Manufacturing Capital Investment (16)
Entrepreneurial Energy	New Companies (11)
	Change in New Companies (48)
	New Business Job Growth (7)
Structural Diversity	Sectoral Diversity (28)
	Dynamic Diversity (37)

DEVELOPMENT CAPACITY INDEX MEASURES

Human Resources	High School Graduation (35)
	High School Education Attainment (13)
	College Education Attainment (14)
Technology Resources	Ph.D. Scientists & Engineers in Workforce (24)
	Science/Engineering Graduate Students (29)
	Patents Issued (19)
	University Research & Development (27)
	Federal Research & Development (34)
	SBIR Grants (11)
Financial Resources	Commercial Bank Deposits (43)
	Loans to Deposits (13)
	Loans to Equity (12)
	Commercial & Industrial Loans (16)
	Comm. & Ind. Loans to Total Loans (12)
	Venture Capital Investments (16)
	SBIC Financings (1)
Infrastructure & Amenity Resources	Highway Deficiency (41)
	Bridge Deficiency (15)
	Urban Mass Transit Availability (10)
	Energy Cost (6)
	Sewage Treatment Needs (38)
	Urban Housing Costs (32)
	Health Professional Shortage Areas (17)
	Tourism Spending (27)

TAX & FISCAL SYSTEM INDEX MEASURES

	Total Tax & Fiscal System Score (38)
	Fiscal Stability & Balanced Revenue (43)
	Tax Fairness (7)
	Fiscal Equalization (44)

PENNSYLVANIA 1994 REPORT CARD

ECONOMIC PERFORMANCE	B
Employment	D
Earnings & Job Quality	A
Equity	C

BUSINESS VITALITY	B
Business Competitiveness	B
Entrepreneurial Energy	F
Structural Diversity	A

DEVELOPMENT CAPACITY	B
Human Resources	C
Technology Resources	B
Financial Resources	A
Infrastructure & Amenity Resources	C

Tax & Fiscal System	√

- **Economic Performance:** Despite already weak and worsening employment figures, Pennsylvania's grade improved one letter from last year, led by job quality measures that are among the best in the nation. Pennsylvania also benefits from below average poverty and above average income distribution.

- **Business Vitality:** Pennsylvania's economy scores high on structural diversity and its businesses, led by a low rate of business closings, show good competitiveness. However, the state's entrepreneurial energy is the worst in the nation.

- **Development Capacity:** Led by solid financial resources, Pennsylvania's development resources are strong. The state's technology resources receive an above average grade, human resources rate only average, and the state's all-important high school graduation rate is among the nation's top twenty.

Five Year Grade Trends

	1990	1991	1992	1993	1994
A					
B					
C					
D					
F					

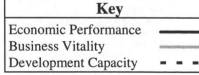

Key

Economic Performance ———
Business Vitality ▨▨▨▨
Development Capacity - - -

For more information on how grades and ranks are calculated, see the Methodology section.
For a detailed explanation of indexes, refer to the individual index section.

WHERE PENNSYLVANIA RANKS – MEASURE BY MEASURE

Scale (top): 50th · 40th · 30th · 20th · 10th · 1st

ECONOMIC PERFORMANCE INDEX MEASURES

Employment
- Long-Term Employment Growth (35)
- Short-Term Employment Growth (36)
- Unemployment Rate (32)
- Unemployment Duration (37)

Earnings & Job Quality
- Average Annual Pay (11)
- Average Annual Pay Growth (11)
- Health Coverage (5)

Equity
- Poverty Rate (20)
- Income Distribution (20)
- Income Distribution Change (33)
- Rural/Urban Disparity (27)

Environmental, Social & Health Conditions
- Air Quality (41)
- Superfund Dumpsites (39)
- Hazardous Waste Generation (26)
- Surface Water Discharge (33)
- Infant Mortality (24)
- Crime Rate (6)
- Teen Pregnancy (14)
- Heart Disease (41)
- Cancer Cases (48)
- Infectious Diseases (23)

BUSINESS VITALITY INDEX MEASURES

Competitiveness of Existing Business
- Traded Sector Strength (19)
- Change in Traded Sector Strength (24)
- Business Closings (12)
- Manufacturing Capital Investment (30)

Entrepreneurial Energy
- New Companies (45)
- Change in New Companies (49)
- New Business Job Growth (33)

Structural Diversity
- Sectoral Diversity (3)
- Dynamic Diversity (11)

DEVELOPMENT CAPACITY INDEX MEASURES

Human Resources
- High School Graduation (17)
- High School Education Attainment (32)
- College Education Attainment (32)

Technology Resources
- Ph.D. Scientists & Engineers in Workforce (20)
- Science/Engineering Graduate Students (22)
- Patents Issued (15)
- University Research & Development (16)
- Federal Research & Development (16)
- SBIR Grants (23)

Financial Resources
- Commercial Bank Deposits (7)
- Loans to Deposits (17)
- Loans to Equity (15)
- Commercial & Industrial Loans (6)
- Comm. & Ind. Loans to Total Loans (7)
- Venture Capital Investments (22)
- SBIC Financings (31)

Infrastructure & Amenity Resources
- Highway Deficiency (26)
- Bridge Deficiency (43)
- Urban Mass Transit Availability (8)
- Energy Cost (38)
- Sewage Treatment Needs (20)
- Urban Housing Costs (30)
- Health Professional Shortage Areas (10)
- Tourism Spending (41)

TAX & FISCAL SYSTEM INDEX MEASURES
- Total Tax & Fiscal System Score (32)
- Fiscal Stability & Balanced Revenue (10)
- Tax Fairness (23)
- Fiscal Equalization (47)

Scale (bottom): 50th · 40th · 30th · 20th · 10th · 1st

RHODE ISLAND 1994 REPORT CARD

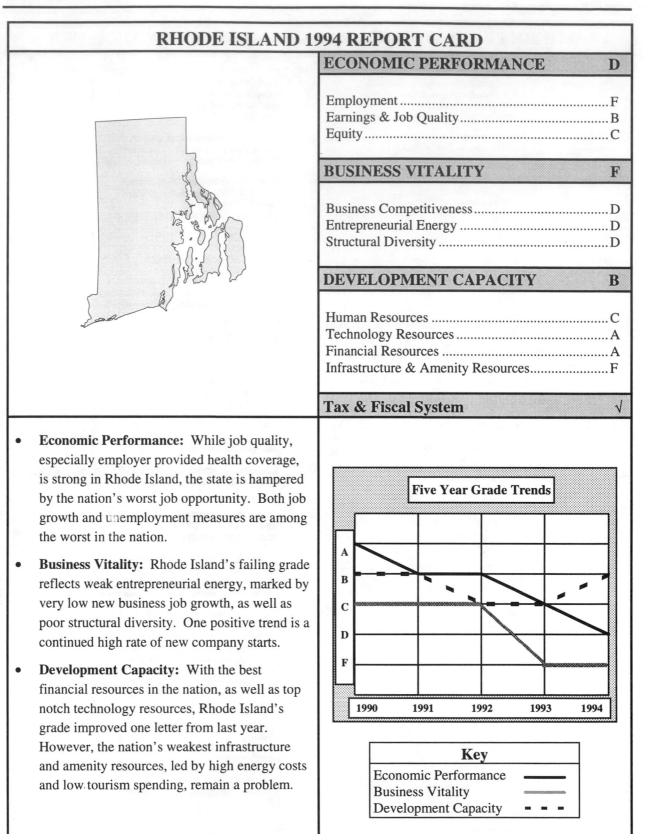

ECONOMIC PERFORMANCE	D

Employment .... F
Earnings & Job Quality .... B
Equity C

BUSINESS VITALITY	F

Business Competitiveness .... D
Entrepreneurial Energy .... D
Structural Diversity .... D

DEVELOPMENT CAPACITY	B

Human Resources C
Technology Resources .... A
Financial Resources .... A
Infrastructure & Amenity Resources .... F

Tax & Fiscal System	√

- **Economic Performance:** While job quality, especially employer provided health coverage, is strong in Rhode Island, the state is hampered by the nation's worst job opportunity. Both job growth and unemployment measures are among the worst in the nation.

- **Business Vitality:** Rhode Island's failing grade reflects weak entrepreneurial energy, marked by very low new business job growth, as well as poor structural diversity. One positive trend is a continued high rate of new company starts.

- **Development Capacity:** With the best financial resources in the nation, as well as top notch technology resources, Rhode Island's grade improved one letter from last year. However, the nation's weakest infrastructure and amenity resources, led by high energy costs and low tourism spending, remain a problem.

Five Year Grade Trends

1990 1991 1992 1993 1994

Key
Economic Performance ——
Business Vitality ▧▧▧
Development Capacity – – –

For more information on how grades and ranks are calculated, see the Methodology section.
For a detailed explanation of indexes, refer to the individual index section.

WHERE RHODE ISLAND RANKS – MEASURE BY MEASURE

Scale (top and bottom): 50th 40th 30th 20th 10th 1st

ECONOMIC PERFORMANCE INDEX MEASURES

Employment
- Long-Term Employment Growth (46)
- Short-Term Employment Growth (47)
- Unemployment Rate (46)
- Unemployment Duration (48)

Earnings & Job Quality
- Average Annual Pay (22)
- Average Annual Pay Growth (19)
- Health Coverage (10)

Equity
- Poverty Rate (23)
- Income Distribution (28)
- Income Distribution Change (46)
- Rural/Urban Disparity (18)

Environmental, Social & Health Conditions
- Air Quality (43)
- Superfund Dumpsites (45)
- Hazardous Waste Generation (7)
- Surface Water Discharge (1)
- Infant Mortality (29)
- Crime Rate (16)
- Teen Pregnancy (12)
- Heart Disease (24)
- Cancer Cases (46)
- Infectious Diseases (18)

BUSINESS VITALITY INDEX MEASURES

Competitiveness of Existing Business
- Traded Sector Strength (32)
- Change in Traded Sector Strength (36)
- Business Closings (12)
- Manufacturing Capital Investment (47)

Entrepreneurial Energy
- New Companies (12)
- Change in New Companies (41)
- New Business Job Growth (48)

Structural Diversity
- Sectoral Diversity (22)
- Dynamic Diversity (45)

DEVELOPMENT CAPACITY INDEX MEASURES

Human Resources
- High School Graduation (32)
- High School Education Attainment (40)
- College Education Attainment (14)

Technology Resources
- Ph.D. Scientists & Engineers in Workforce (7)
- Science/Engineering Graduate Students (5)
- Patents Issued (17)
- University Research & Development (8)
- Federal Research & Development (8)
- SBIR Grants (15)

Financial Resources
- Commercial Bank Deposits (14)
- Loans to Deposits (3)
- Loans to Equity (3)
- Commercial & Industrial Loans (2)
- Comm. & Ind. Loans to Total Loans (1)
- Venture Capital Investments (11)
- SBIC Financings (4)

Infrastructure & Amenity Resources
- Highway Deficiency (49)
- Bridge Deficiency (44)
- Urban Mass Transit Availability (14)
- Energy Cost (50)
- Sewage Treatment Needs (47)
- Urban Housing Costs (48)
- Health Professional Shortage Areas (31)
- Tourism Spending (50)

TAX & FISCAL SYSTEM INDEX MEASURES

- Total Tax & Fiscal System Score (34)
- Fiscal Stability & Balanced Revenue (21)
- Tax Fairness (28)
- Fiscal Equalization (40)

SOUTH CAROLINA 1994 REPORT CARD

ECONOMIC PERFORMANCE	D
Employment	C
Earnings & Job Quality	D
Equity	C

BUSINESS VITALITY	D
Business Competitiveness	C
Entrepreneurial Energy	F
Structural Diversity	C

DEVELOPMENT CAPACITY	D
Human Resources	F
Technology Resources	D
Financial Resources	D
Infrastructure & Amenity Resources	B

Tax & Fiscal System	+

- **Economic Performance:** South Carolina's poor grade reflects a worsening employment picture, marked by a sharp increase in unemployment and slowing in job growth, and continued weakness in earnings and job quality. Although the poverty rate has increased, the state benefits from improved rank in income distribution.

- **Business Vitality:** Although improved from last year, vitality in South Carolina is still weak, marked by the second lowest level of entrepreneurial energy in the U.S. One plus is high manufacturing capital investment.

- **Development Capacity:** With strong highways, bridges, and sewage treatment, and low energy costs, South Carolina has the second best infrastructure resources in the South. However, with the nation's third worst high school graduation rate, the state's human resources earn a failing mark. Financial and technology resources are also weak.

Five Year Grade Trends

	1990	1991	1992	1993	1994

Key
Economic Performance ———
Business Vitality ▓▓▓▓▓
Development Capacity – – –

For more information on how grades and ranks are calculated, see the Methodology section.
For a detailed explanation of indexes, refer to the individual index section.

WHERE SOUTH CAROLINA RANKS – MEASURE BY MEASURE

50th   40th   30th   20th   10th   1st

ECONOMIC PERFORMANCE INDEX MEASURES

Employment
Long-Term Employment Growth (16)
Short-Term Employment Growth (38)
Unemployment Rate (41)
Unemployment Duration (26)

Earnings & Job Quality
Average Annual Pay (40)
Average Annual Pay Growth (31)
Health Coverage (41)

Equity
Poverty Rate (45)
Income Distribution (31)
Income Distribution Change (15)
Rural/Urban Disparity (12)

Environmental, Social & Health Conditions
Air Quality (13)
Superfund Dumpsites (33)
Hazardous Waste Generation (29)
Surface Water Discharge (31)
Infant Mortality (41)
Crime Rate (38)
Teen Pregnancy (38)
Heart Disease (39)
Cancer Cases (15)
Infectious Diseases (30)

BUSINESS VITALITY INDEX MEASURES

Competitiveness of Existing Business
Traded Sector Strength (33)
Change in Traded Sector Strength (44)
Business Closings (22)
Manufacturing Capital Investment (10)

Entrepreneurial Energy
New Companies (40)
Change in New Companies (47)
New Business Job Growth (38)

Structural Diversity
Sectoral Diversity (32)
Dynamic Diversity (17)

DEVELOPMENT CAPACITY INDEX MEASURES

Human Resources
High School Graduation (48)
High School Education Attainment (46)
College Education Attainment (39)

Technology Resources
Ph.D. Scientists & Engineers in Workforce (40)
Science/Engineering Graduate Students (40)
Patents Issued (31)
University Research & Development (42)
Federal Research & Development (36)
SBIR Grants (50)

Financial Resources
Commercial Bank Deposits (48)
Loans to Deposits (22)
Loans to Equity (14)
Commercial & Industrial Loans (45)
Comm. & Ind. Loans to Total Loans (40)
Venture Capital Investments (34)
SBIC Financings (25)

Infrastructure & Amenity Resources
Highway Deficiency (16)
Bridge Deficiency (4)
Urban Mass Transit Availability (40)
Energy Cost (14)
Sewage Treatment Needs (12)
Urban Housing Costs (22)
Health Professional Shortage Areas (44)
Tourism Spending (17)

TAX & FISCAL SYSTEM INDEX MEASURES

Total Tax & Fiscal System Score (10)
Fiscal Stability & Balanced Revenue (2)
Tax Fairness (22)
Fiscal Equalization (22)

50th   40th   30th   20th   10th   1st

SOUTH DAKOTA 1994 REPORT CARD

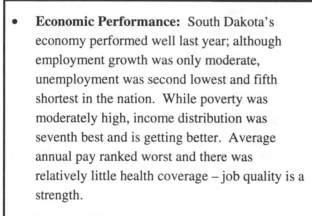

ECONOMIC PERFORMANCE	B
Employment	B
Earnings & Job Quality	D
Equity	A

BUSINESS VITALITY	D
Business Competitiveness	B
Entrepreneurial Energy	C
Structural Diversity	D

DEVELOPMENT CAPACITY	D
Human Resources	C
Technology Resources	F
Financial Resources	B
Infrastructure & Amenity Resources	C

Tax & Fiscal System	–

- **Economic Performance:** South Dakota's economy performed well last year; although employment growth was only moderate, unemployment was second lowest and fifth shortest in the nation. While poverty was moderately high, income distribution was seventh best and is getting better. Average annual pay ranked worst and there was relatively little health coverage – job quality is a strength.

- **Business Vitality:** South Dakota's economy is poorly diversified but its existing businesses are competitive. There were few business closings and a large increase in traded sector strength.

- **Development Capacity:** South Dakota is lacking in some resources needed to expand and diversify. Although human resources are only slightly below the median, technology resources are dismal with the low federal R&D, poor university R&D, and few patents. Only financial resources are strong, led by high deposits and commercial and industrial loans.

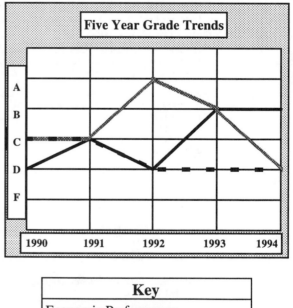

Five Year Grade Trends

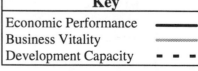

Key	
Economic Performance	——
Business Vitality	~~~~
Development Capacity	- - -

For more information on how grades and ranks are calculated, see the Methodology section.
For a detailed explanation of indexes, refer to the individual index section.

WHERE SOUTH DAKOTA RANKS – MEASURE BY MEASURE

Scale: 50th 40th 30th 20th 10th 1st

ECONOMIC PERFORMANCE INDEX MEASURES

Employment
- Long-Term Employment Growth (40)
- Short-Term Employment Growth (30)
- Unemployment Rate (2)
- Unemployment Duration (5)

Earnings & Job Quality
- Average Annual Pay (50)
- Average Annual Pay Growth (26)
- Health Coverage (42)

Equity
- Poverty Rate (30)
- Income Distribution (7)
- Income Distribution Change (2)
- Rural/Urban Disparity (34)

Environmental, Social & Health Conditions
- Air Quality (1)
- Superfund Dumpsites (29)
- Hazardous Waste Generation (1)
- Surface Water Discharge (23)
- Infant Mortality (44)
- Crime Rate (3)
- Teen Pregnancy (14)
- Heart Disease (21)
- Cancer Cases (23)
- Infectious Diseases (44)

BUSINESS VITALITY INDEX MEASURES

Competitiveness of Existing Business
- Traded Sector Strength (37)
- Change in Traded Sector Strength (5)
- Business Closings (10)
- Manufacturing Capital Investment (37)

Entrepreneurial Energy
- New Companies (29)
- Change in New Companies (33)
- New Business Job Growth (22)

Structural Diversity
- Sectoral Diversity (48)
- Dynamic Diversity (28)

DEVELOPMENT CAPACITY INDEX MEASURES

Human Resources
- High School Graduation (6)
- High School Education Attainment (35)
- College Education Attainment (32)

Technology Resources
- Ph.D. Scientists & Engineers in Workforce (38)
- Science/Engineering Graduate Students (21)
- Patents Issued (49)
- University Research & Development (48)
- Federal Research & Development (50)
- SBIR Grants (47)

Financial Resources
- Commercial Bank Deposits (2)
- Loans to Deposits (2)
- Loans to Equity (29)
- Commercial & Industrial Loans (3)
- Comm. & Ind. Loans to Total Loans (35)
- Venture Capital Investments (37)
- SBIC Financing (44)

Infrastructure & Amenity Resources
- Highway Deficiency (31)
- Bridge Deficiency (22)
- Urban Mass Transit Availability (47)
- Energy Cost (21)
- Sewage Treatment Needs (10)
- Urban Housing Costs (7)
- Health Professional Shortage Areas (49)
- Tourism Spending (26)

TAX & FISCAL SYSTEM INDEX MEASURES

- Total Tax & Fiscal System Score (50)
- Fiscal Stability & Balanced Revenue (41)
- Tax Fairness (50)
- Fiscal Equalization (46)

Scale: 50th 40th 30th 20th 10th 1st

TENNESSEE 1994 REPORT CARD

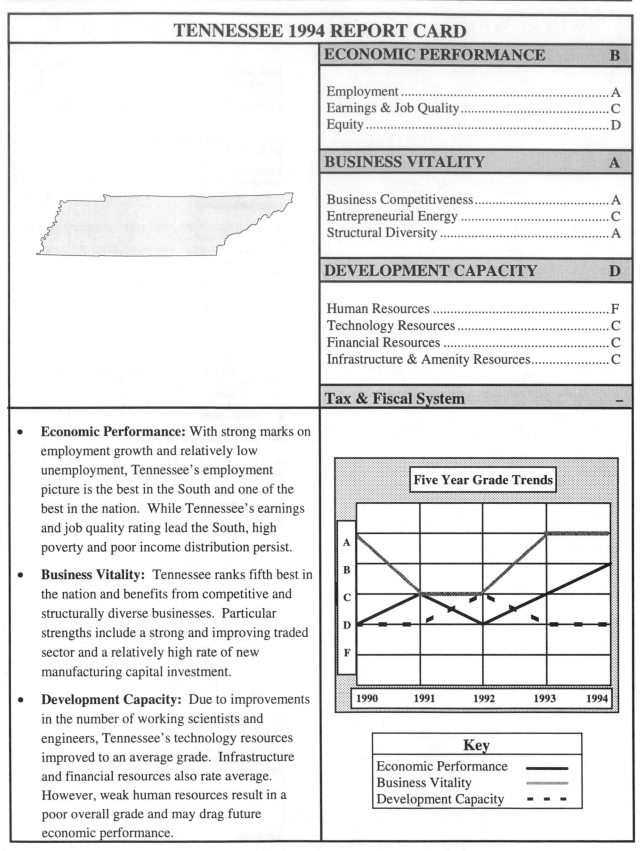

ECONOMIC PERFORMANCE	B
Employment	A
Earnings & Job Quality	C
Equity	D

BUSINESS VITALITY	A
Business Competitiveness	A
Entrepreneurial Energy	C
Structural Diversity	A

DEVELOPMENT CAPACITY	D
Human Resources	F
Technology Resources	C
Financial Resources	C
Infrastructure & Amenity Resources	C

Tax & Fiscal System	–

Five Year Grade Trends

Key
Economic Performance ——
Business Vitality
Development Capacity - - -

- **Economic Performance:** With strong marks on employment growth and relatively low unemployment, Tennessee's employment picture is the best in the South and one of the best in the nation. While Tennessee's earnings and job quality rating lead the South, high poverty and poor income distribution persist.

- **Business Vitality:** Tennessee ranks fifth best in the nation and benefits from competitive and structurally diverse businesses. Particular strengths include a strong and improving traded sector and a relatively high rate of new manufacturing capital investment.

- **Development Capacity:** Due to improvements in the number of working scientists and engineers, Tennessee's technology resources improved to an average grade. Infrastructure and financial resources also rate average. However, weak human resources result in a poor overall grade and may drag future economic performance.

For more information on how grades and ranks are calculated, see the Methodology section.
For a detailed explanation of indexes, refer to the individual index section.

WHERE TENNESSEE RANKS – MEASURE BY MEASURE

50th 40th 30th 20th 10th 1st

ECONOMIC PERFORMANCE INDEX MEASURES

Employment
- Long-Term Employment Growth (20)
- Short-Term Employment Growth (16)
- Unemployment Rate (17)
- Unemployment Duration (11)

Earnings & Job Quality
- Average Annual Pay (29)
- Average Annual Pay Growth (8)
- Health Coverage (34)

Equity
- Poverty Rate (39)
- Income Distribution (38)
- Income Distribution Change (18)
- Rural/Urban Disparity (23)

Environmental, Social & Health Conditions
- Air Quality (27)
- Superfund Dumpsites (14)
- Hazardous Waste Generation (34)
- Surface Water Discharge (19)
- Infant Mortality (35)
- Crime Rate (27)
- Teen Pregnancy (40)
- Heart Disease (43)
- Cancer Cases (36)
- Infectious Diseases (36)

BUSINESS VITALITY INDEX MEASURES

Competitiveness of Existing Business
- Traded Sector Strength (18)
- Change in Traded Sector Strength (10)
- Business Closings (33)
- Manufacturing Capital Investment (11)

Entrepreneurial Energy
- New Companies (30)
- Change in New Companies (27)
- New Business Job Growth (24)

Structural Diversity
- Sectoral Diversity (4)
- Dynamic Diversity (26)

DEVELOPMENT CAPACITY INDEX MEASURES

Human Resources
- High School Graduation (41)
- High School Education Attainment (46)
- College Education Attainment (45)

Technology Resources
- Ph.D. Scientists & Engineers in Workforce (28)
- Science/Engineering Graduate Students (39)
- Patents Issued (38)
- University Research & Development (38)
- Federal Research & Development (21)
- SBIR Grants (27)

Financial Resources
- Commercial Bank Deposits (20)
- Loans to Deposits (33)
- Loans to Equity (27)
- Commercial & Industrial Loans (25)
- Comm. & Ind. Loans to Total Loans (21)
- Venture Capital Investments (26)
- SBIC Financings (24)

Infrastructure & Amenity Resources
- Highway Deficiency (39)
- Bridge Deficiency (27)
- Urban Mass Transit Availability (30)
- Energy Cost (9)
- Sewage Treatment Needs (35)
- Urban Housing Costs (10)
- Health Professional Shortage Areas (32)
- Tourism Spending (9)

TAX & FISCAL SYSTEM INDEX MEASURES

- Total Tax & Fiscal System Score (45)
- Fiscal Stability & Balanced Revenue (37)
- Tax Fairness (46)
- Fiscal Equalization (33)

50th 40th 30th 20th 10th 1st

TEXAS 1994 REPORT CARD

ECONOMIC PERFORMANCE	C
Employment	C
Earnings & Job Quality	C
Equity	C

BUSINESS VITALITY	A
Business Competitiveness	B
Entrepreneurial Energy	A
Structural Diversity	A

DEVELOPMENT CAPACITY	C
Human Resources	D
Technology Resources	C
Financial Resources	C
Infrastructure & Amenity Resources	B

Tax & Fiscal System	–

- **Economic Performance:** Texas' average grade reflects uneven economic performance. While job opportunities are above average, unemployment is relatively high. Average pay is good, but health coverage is poor. The change in income distribution is a positive trend, however the poverty rate is still high.

- **Business Vitality:** Texas leads the nation in business vitality. The state has one of the most structurally diverse economies, a high degree of entrepreneurial energy, and strongly competitive industries supported by relatively high new manufacturing capital investment.

- **Development Capacity:** Texas' average grade reflects a mixed bag of development resources. With top twenty rankings for highways, bridges, and urban mass transit, the state's infrastructure resources are strong. However, technology and financial resources are only average, and human resources are the weakest in the Plains region.

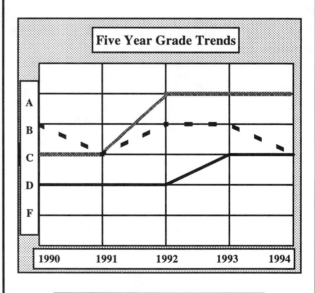

Five Year Grade Trends

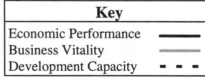

Key	
Economic Performance	———
Business Vitality	▬▬▬
Development Capacity	- - -

For more information on how grades and ranks are calculated, see the Methodology section.
For a detailed explanation of indexes, refer to the individual index section.

WHERE TEXAS RANKS – MEASURE BY MEASURE

Scale across top and bottom: 50th · 40th · 30th · 20th · 10th · 1st

ECONOMIC PERFORMANCE INDEX MEASURES

Employment
- Long-Term Employment Growth (22)
- Short-Term Employment Growth (20)
- Unemployment Rate (32)
- Unemployment Duration (21)

Earnings & Job Quality
- Average Annual Pay (15)
- Average Annual Pay Growth (13)
- Health Coverage (44)

Equity
- Poverty Rate (42)
- Income Distribution (43)
- Income Distribution Change (16)
- Rural/Urban Disparity (7)

Environmental, Social & Health Conditions
- Air Quality (38)
- Superfund Dumpsites (3)
- Hazardous Waste Generation (48)
- Surface Water Discharge (37)
- Infant Mortality (11)
- Crime Rate (49)
- Teen Pregnancy (46)
- Heart Disease (27)
- Cancer Cases (6)
- Infectious Diseases (40)

BUSINESS VITALITY INDEX MEASURES

Competitiveness of Existing Business
- Traded Sector Strength (25)
- Change in Traded Sector Strength (13)
- Business Closings (41)
- Manufacturing Capital Investment (5)

Entrepreneurial Energy
- New Companies (21)
- Change in New Companies (23)
- New Business Job Growth (14)

Structural Diversity
- Sectoral Diversity (14)
- Dynamic Diversity (1)

DEVELOPMENT CAPACITY INDEX MEASURES

Human Resources
- High School Graduation (43)
- High School Education Attainment (35)
- College Education Attainment (23)

Technology Resources
- Ph.D. Scientists & Engineers in Workforce (31)
- Science/Engineering Graduate Students (20)
- Patents Issued (22)
- University Research & Development (22)
- Federal Research & Development (23)
- SBIR Grants (31)

Financial Resources
- Commercial Bank Deposits (31)
- Loans to Deposits (43)
- Loans to Equity (38)
- Commercial & Industrial Loans (22)
- Comm. & Ind. Loans to Total Loans (8)
- Venture Capital Investments (19)
- SBIC Financings (17)

Infrastructure & Amenity Resources
- Highway Deficiency (15)
- Bridge Deficiency (13)
- Urban Mass Transit Availability (19)
- Energy Cost (25)
- Sewage Treatment Needs (22)
- Urban Housing Costs (34)
- Health Professional Shortage Areas (25)
- Tourism Spending (21)

TAX & FISCAL SYSTEM INDEX MEASURES

- Total Tax & Fiscal System Score (48)
- Fiscal Stability & Balanced Revenue (44)
- Tax Fairness (47)
- Fiscal Equalization (31)

UTAH 1994 REPORT CARD

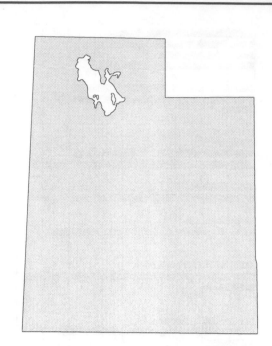

ECONOMIC PERFORMANCE	A

Employment .... A
Earnings & Job Quality .... B
Equity .... A

BUSINESS VITALITY	B

Business Competitiveness .... D
Entrepreneurial Energy .... A
Structural Diversity .... B

DEVELOPMENT CAPACITY	A

Human Resources .... A
Technology Resources .... A
Financial Resources .... D
Infrastructure & Amenity Resources .... A

Tax & Fiscal System	+

- **Economic Performance:** Like most of the Mountain West, Utah's economy has been growing rapidly. Short- and long-term employment growth are in the top ten and unemployment duration is the second shortest. Annual pay is very low but improving moderately well. Wages need to be better to improve the state's low equity.

- **Business Vitality:** Utah's vitality grade improved one letter from last year, led by continued high levels of entrepreneurial energy. Yet, with a high rate of business closings and a weak traded sector, the competitiveness of the state's businesses remains a problem.

- **Development Capacity:** With the highest grades for its human, technology, and infrastructure and amenity resources, Utah has the nation's fourth best development resources. The state's only weakness is its poor financial resources.

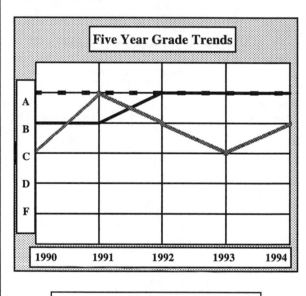

Five Year Grade Trends

	1990	1991	1992	1993	1994
A					
B					
C					
D					
F					

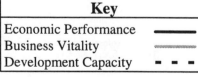

Key	
Economic Performance	———
Business Vitality	~~~~~
Development Capacity	- - -

For more information on how grades and ranks are calculated, see the Methodology section.
For a detailed explanation of indexes, refer to the individual index section.

WHERE UTAH RANKS – MEASURE BY MEASURE

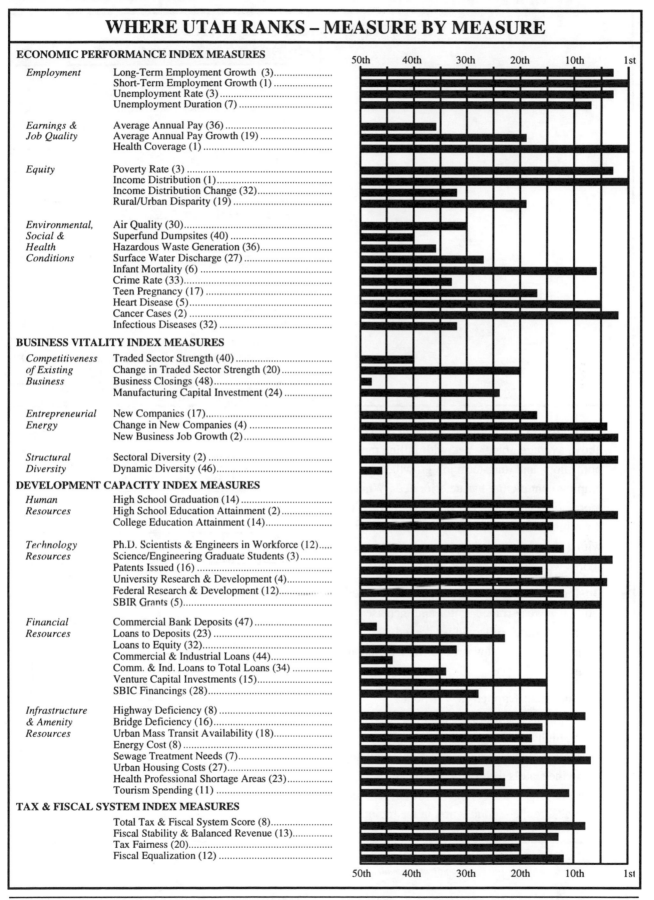

ECONOMIC PERFORMANCE INDEX MEASURES

		50th	40th	30th	20th	10th	1st

Employment
- Long-Term Employment Growth (3)
- Short-Term Employment Growth (1)
- Unemployment Rate (3)
- Unemployment Duration (7)

Earnings & Job Quality
- Average Annual Pay (36)
- Average Annual Pay Growth (19)
- Health Coverage (1)

Equity
- Poverty Rate (3)
- Income Distribution (1)
- Income Distribution Change (32)
- Rural/Urban Disparity (19)

Environmental, Social & Health Conditions
- Air Quality (30)
- Superfund Dumpsites (40)
- Hazardous Waste Generation (36)
- Surface Water Discharge (27)
- Infant Mortality (6)
- Crime Rate (33)
- Teen Pregnancy (17)
- Heart Disease (5)
- Cancer Cases (2)
- Infectious Diseases (32)

BUSINESS VITALITY INDEX MEASURES

Competitiveness of Existing Business
- Traded Sector Strength (40)
- Change in Traded Sector Strength (20)
- Business Closings (48)
- Manufacturing Capital Investment (24)

Entrepreneurial Energy
- New Companies (17)
- Change in New Companies (4)
- New Business Job Growth (2)

Structural Diversity
- Sectoral Diversity (2)
- Dynamic Diversity (46)

DEVELOPMENT CAPACITY INDEX MEASURES

Human Resources
- High School Graduation (14)
- High School Education Attainment (2)
- College Education Attainment (14)

Technology Resources
- Ph.D. Scientists & Engineers in Workforce (12)
- Science/Engineering Graduate Students (3)
- Patents Issued (16)
- University Research & Development (4)
- Federal Research & Development (12)
- SBIR Grants (5)

Financial Resources
- Commercial Bank Deposits (47)
- Loans to Deposits (23)
- Loans to Equity (32)
- Commercial & Industrial Loans (44)
- Comm. & Ind. Loans to Total Loans (34)
- Venture Capital Investments (15)
- SBIC Financings (28)

Infrastructure & Amenity Resources
- Highway Deficiency (8)
- Bridge Deficiency (16)
- Urban Mass Transit Availability (18)
- Energy Cost (8)
- Sewage Treatment Needs (7)
- Urban Housing Costs (27)
- Health Professional Shortage Areas (23)
- Tourism Spending (11)

TAX & FISCAL SYSTEM INDEX MEASURES
- Total Tax & Fiscal System Score (8)
- Fiscal Stability & Balanced Revenue (13)
- Tax Fairness (20)
- Fiscal Equalization (12)

		50th	40th	30th	20th	10th	1st

VERMONT 1994 REPORT CARD

ECONOMIC PERFORMANCE	B
Employment	C
Earnings & Job Quality	C
Equity	B

BUSINESS VITALITY	C
Business Competitiveness	D
Entrepreneurial Energy	A
Structural Diversity	C

DEVELOPMENT CAPACITY	C
Human Resources	B
Technology Resources	B
Financial Resources	C
Infrastructure & Amenity Resources	D

Tax & Fiscal System	√

- **Economic Performance:** Vermont earns an above average grade. Yet, with falling ranks for both short- and long-term job growth, the state's employment picture has deteriorated. What's more, job quality remains only average and is the region's second worst. At the same time, with a sharply reduced poverty rate, the state scores well on measures of equity.

- **Business Vitality:** Vermont's grade dropped a letter as a weak traded sector and increased business failures reflected weakened competitiveness. New firm formations remain a strength.

- **Development Capacity:** Vermont's development resources are a mixed bag. With strong high school graduation and college attainment, human resources are above average, as are the state's technology resources. However, the state's financial resources, though average, are the second worst in the region, and infrastructure resources are weak.

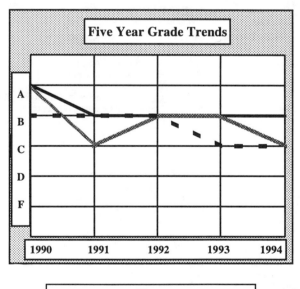

Five Year Grade Trends

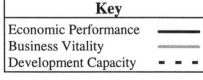

Key	
Economic Performance	———
Business Vitality	～～～
Development Capacity	- - -

For more information on how grades and ranks are calculated, see the Methodology section.
For a detailed explanation of indexes, refer to the individual index section.

WHERE VERMONT RANKS – MEASURE BY MEASURE

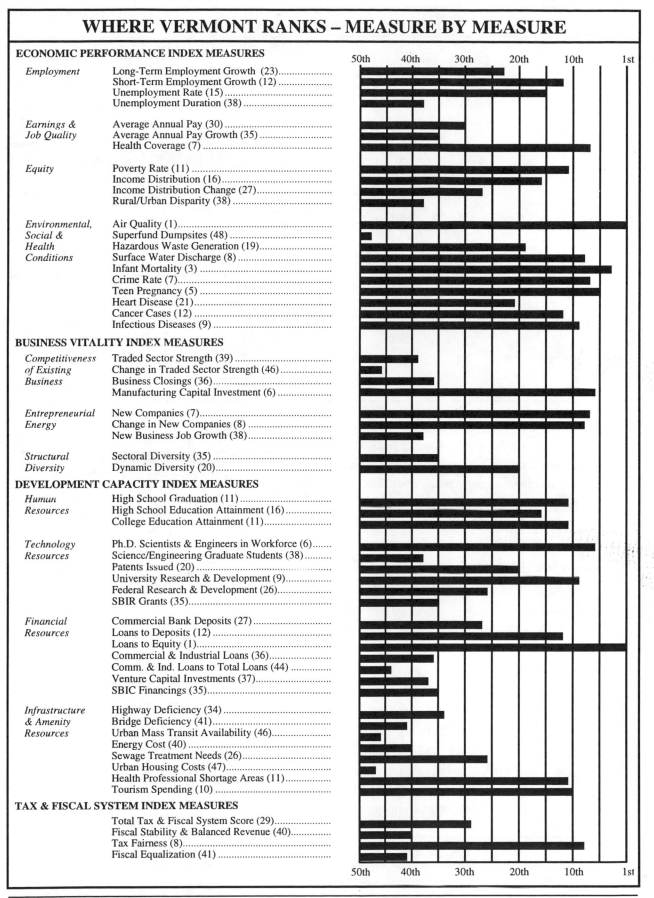

ECONOMIC PERFORMANCE INDEX MEASURES

Employment
Long-Term Employment Growth (23)
Short-Term Employment Growth (12)
Unemployment Rate (15)
Unemployment Duration (38)

Earnings & Job Quality
Average Annual Pay (30)
Average Annual Pay Growth (35)
Health Coverage (7)

Equity
Poverty Rate (11)
Income Distribution (16)
Income Distribution Change (27)
Rural/Urban Disparity (38)

Environmental, Social & Health Conditions
Air Quality (1)
Superfund Dumpsites (48)
Hazardous Waste Generation (19)
Surface Water Discharge (8)
Infant Mortality (3)
Crime Rate (7)
Teen Pregnancy (5)
Heart Disease (21)
Cancer Cases (12)
Infectious Diseases (9)

BUSINESS VITALITY INDEX MEASURES

Competitiveness of Existing Business
Traded Sector Strength (39)
Change in Traded Sector Strength (46)
Business Closings (36)
Manufacturing Capital Investment (6)

Entrepreneurial Energy
New Companies (7)
Change in New Companies (8)
New Business Job Growth (38)

Structural Diversity
Sectoral Diversity (35)
Dynamic Diversity (20)

DEVELOPMENT CAPACITY INDEX MEASURES

Human Resources
High School Graduation (11)
High School Education Attainment (16)
College Education Attainment (11)

Technology Resources
Ph.D. Scientists & Engineers in Workforce (6)
Science/Engineering Graduate Students (38)
Patents Issued (20)
University Research & Development (9)
Federal Research & Development (26)
SBIR Grants (35)

Financial Resources
Commercial Bank Deposits (27)
Loans to Deposits (12)
Loans to Equity (1)
Commercial & Industrial Loans (36)
Comm. & Ind. Loans to Total Loans (44)
Venture Capital Investments (37)
SBIC Financings (35)

Infrastructure & Amenity Resources
Highway Deficiency (34)
Bridge Deficiency (41)
Urban Mass Transit Availability (46)
Energy Cost (40)
Sewage Treatment Needs (26)
Urban Housing Costs (47)
Health Professional Shortage Areas (11)
Tourism Spending (10)

TAX & FISCAL SYSTEM INDEX MEASURES

Total Tax & Fiscal System Score (29)
Fiscal Stability & Balanced Revenue (40)
Tax Fairness (8)
Fiscal Equalization (41)

(chart scale: 50th, 40th, 30th, 20th, 10th, 1st)

VIRGINIA 1994 REPORT CARD

ECONOMIC PERFORMANCE	B
Employment	C
Earnings & Job Quality	C
Equity	B

BUSINESS VITALITY	B
Business Competitiveness	F
Entrepreneurial Energy	C
Structural Diversity	A

DEVELOPMENT CAPACITY	C
Human Resources	C
Technology Resources	B
Financial Resources	C
Infrastructure & Amenity Resources	C

Tax & Fiscal System	–

- **Economic Performance:** Virginia is one of only two Southern states to score better than a C on performance. While employment prospects and job quality are only average in the state, Virginia scores well on measures of equity, led by low poverty and the nation's most improved income distribution.

- **Business Vitality:** Virginia's grade improved one letter from last year, led by the nation's most structurally diverse economy. However, with low new manufacturing capital investment and a weak traded sector, the competitiveness of businesses is poor.

- **Development Capacity:** Although Virginia's development resources receive only an average grade, the state is one of only two Southern states to score better than a D in Capacity. Virginia has strong technology resources, led by high levels of federal R&D spending and SBIR grants, and its human resources are the best in the South.

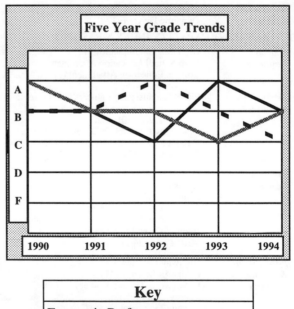

Five Year Grade Trends

1990 1991 1992 1993 1994

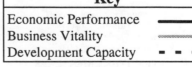

Key	
Economic Performance	
Business Vitality	
Development Capacity	

For more information on how grades and ranks are calculated, see the Methodology section.
For a detailed explanation of indexes, refer to the individual index section.

The Corporation for Enterprise Development

WHERE VIRGINIA RANKS – MEASURE BY MEASURE

	50th	40th	30th	20th	10th	1st

ECONOMIC PERFORMANCE INDEX MEASURES

Employment
- Long-Term Employment Growth (12)
- Short-Term Employment Growth (35)
- Unemployment Rate (9)
- Unemployment Duration (31)

Earnings & Job Quality
- Average Annual Pay (17)
- Average Annual Pay Growth (31)
- Health Coverage (23)

Equity
- Poverty Rate (4)
- Income Distribution (27)
- Income Distribution Change (1)
- Rural/Urban Disparity (43)

Environmental, Social & Health Conditions
- Air Quality (35)
- Superfund Dumpsites (18)
- Hazardous Waste Generation (30)
- Surface Water Discharge (10)
- Infant Mortality (36)
- Crime Rate (12)
- Teen Pregnancy (18)
- Heart Disease (29)
- Cancer Cases (14)
- Infectious Diseases (17)

BUSINESS VITALITY INDEX MEASURES

Competitiveness of Existing Business
- Traded Sector Strength (34)
- Change in Traded Sector Strength (34)
- Business Closings (32)
- Manufacturing Capital Investment (37)

Entrepreneurial Energy
- New Companies (24)
- Change in New Companies (21)
- New Business Job Growth (30)

Structural Diversity
- Sectoral Diversity (1)
- Dynamic Diversity (7)

DEVELOPMENT CAPACITY INDEX MEASURES

Human Resources
- High School Graduation (27)
- High School Education Attainment (32)
- College Education Attainment (7)

Technology Resources
- Ph.D. Scientists & Engineers in Workforce (13)
- Science/Engineering Graduate Students (14)
- Patents Issued (29)
- University Research & Development (32)
- Federal Research & Development (6)
- SBIR Grants (8)

Financial Resources
- Commercial Bank Deposits (23)
- Loans to Deposits (31)
- Loans to Equity (22)
- Commercial & Industrial Loans (32)
- Comm. & Ind. Loans to Total Loans (32)
- Venture Capital Investments (12)
- SBIC Financings (27)

Infrastructure & Amenity Resources
- Highway Deficiency (32)
- Bridge Deficiency (17)
- Urban Mass Transit Availability (33)
- Energy Cost (25)
- Sewage Treatment Needs (40)
- Urban Housing Costs (37)
- Health Professional Shortage Areas (12)
- Tourism Spending (12)

TAX & FISCAL SYSTEM INDEX MEASURES

- Total Tax & Fiscal System Score (42)
- Fiscal Stability & Balanced Revenue (31)
- Tax Fairness (29)
- Fiscal Equalization (43)

	50th	40th	30th	20th	10th	1st

WASHINGTON 1994 REPORT CARD

ECONOMIC PERFORMANCE	B
Employment	C
Earnings & Job Quality	A
Equity	C

BUSINESS VITALITY	C
Business Competitiveness	C
Entrepreneurial Energy	A
Structural Diversity	F

DEVELOPMENT CAPACITY	A
Human Resources	A
Technology Resources	B
Financial Resources	B
Infrastructure & Amenity Resources	A

Tax & Fiscal System	–

- **Economic Performance:** Due to a worsening short-term employment picture and a declining rank in the change in income distribution, the state's grade dropped a letter grade from last year. However, job quality in the state is top notch and long-term employment growth is second in the nation. Low ranks on several environmental measures are a lingering problem.

- **Business Vitality:** Washington's average grade on business vitality reflects the nation's highest level of entrepreneurial energy, combined with only average competitiveness and very poor structural diversity.

- **Development Capacity:** As it has for the last five years, Washington earned an excellent grade for its development resources. The state's infrastructure and human resources are tops in the region and its technology and infrastructure resources are also strong.

Five Year Grade Trends

A B C D F

1990 1991 1992 1993 1994

Key	
Economic Performance	——
Business Vitality	∼∼∼
Development Capacity	- - -

For more information on how grades and ranks are calculated, see the Methodology section.
For a detailed explanation of indexes, refer to the individual index section.

WHERE WASHINGTON RANKS – MEASURE BY MEASURE

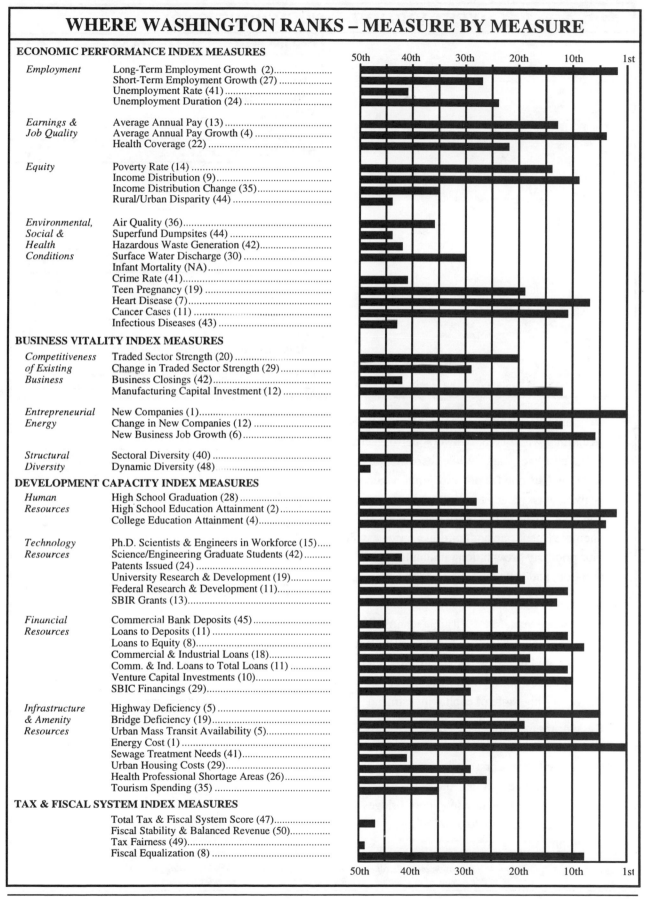

ECONOMIC PERFORMANCE INDEX MEASURES

Employment
- Long-Term Employment Growth (2)
- Short-Term Employment Growth (27)
- Unemployment Rate (41)
- Unemployment Duration (24)

Earnings & Job Quality
- Average Annual Pay (13)
- Average Annual Pay Growth (4)
- Health Coverage (22)

Equity
- Poverty Rate (14)
- Income Distribution (9)
- Income Distribution Change (35)
- Rural/Urban Disparity (44)

Environmental, Social & Health Conditions
- Air Quality (36)
- Superfund Dumpsites (44)
- Hazardous Waste Generation (42)
- Surface Water Discharge (30)
- Infant Mortality (NA)
- Crime Rate (41)
- Teen Pregnancy (19)
- Heart Disease (7)
- Cancer Cases (11)
- Infectious Diseases (43)

BUSINESS VITALITY INDEX MEASURES

Competitiveness of Existing Business
- Traded Sector Strength (20)
- Change in Traded Sector Strength (29)
- Business Closings (42)
- Manufacturing Capital Investment (12)

Entrepreneurial Energy
- New Companies (1)
- Change in New Companies (12)
- New Business Job Growth (6)

Structural Diversity
- Sectoral Diversity (40)
- Dynamic Diversity (48)

DEVELOPMENT CAPACITY INDEX MEASURES

Human Resources
- High School Graduation (28)
- High School Education Attainment (2)
- College Education Attainment (4)

Technology Resources
- Ph.D. Scientists & Engineers in Workforce (15)
- Science/Engineering Graduate Students (42)
- Patents Issued (24)
- University Research & Development (19)
- Federal Research & Development (11)
- SBIR Grants (13)

Financial Resources
- Commercial Bank Deposits (45)
- Loans to Deposits (11)
- Loans to Equity (8)
- Commercial & Industrial Loans (18)
- Comm. & Ind. Loans to Total Loans (11)
- Venture Capital Investments (10)
- SBIC Financings (29)

Infrastructure & Amenity Resources
- Highway Deficiency (5)
- Bridge Deficiency (19)
- Urban Mass Transit Availability (5)
- Energy Cost (1)
- Sewage Treatment Needs (41)
- Urban Housing Costs (29)
- Health Professional Shortage Areas (26)
- Tourism Spending (35)

TAX & FISCAL SYSTEM INDEX MEASURES
- Total Tax & Fiscal System Score (47)
- Fiscal Stability & Balanced Revenue (50)
- Tax Fairness (49)
- Fiscal Equalization (8)

Scale: 50th — 40th — 30th — 20th — 10th — 1st

WEST VIRGINIA 1994 REPORT CARD

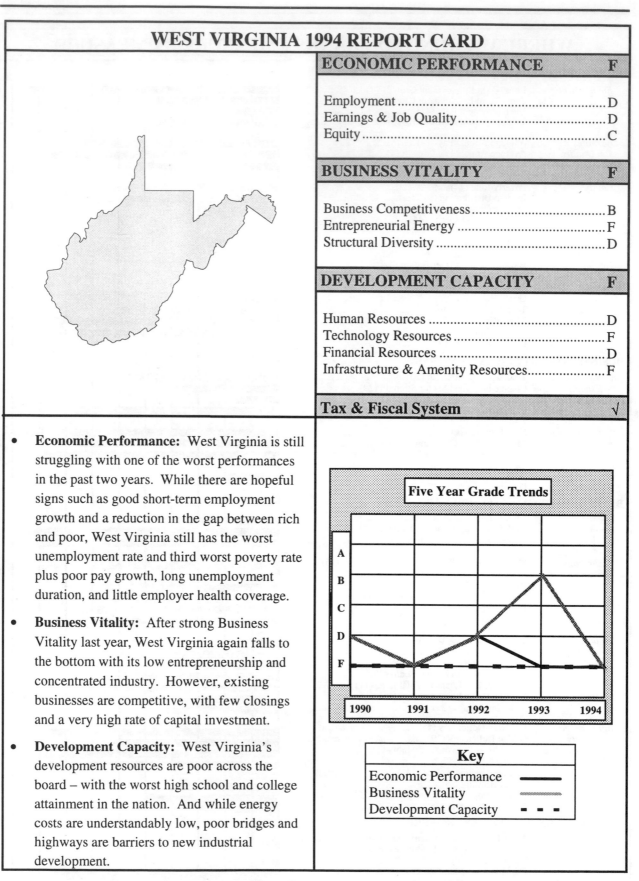

ECONOMIC PERFORMANCE	F
Employment	D
Earnings & Job Quality	D
Equity	C

BUSINESS VITALITY	F
Business Competitiveness	B
Entrepreneurial Energy	F
Structural Diversity	D

DEVELOPMENT CAPACITY	F
Human Resources	D
Technology Resources	F
Financial Resources	D
Infrastructure & Amenity Resources	F

Tax & Fiscal System	√

Five Year Grade Trends

(Grade scale A, B, C, D, F plotted for years 1990, 1991, 1992, 1993, 1994)

Key

Economic Performance	——
Business Vitality	~~~~
Development Capacity	– – –

- **Economic Performance:** West Virginia is still struggling with one of the worst performances in the past two years. While there are hopeful signs such as good short-term employment growth and a reduction in the gap between rich and poor, West Virginia still has the worst unemployment rate and third worst poverty rate plus poor pay growth, long unemployment duration, and little employer health coverage.

- **Business Vitality:** After strong Business Vitality last year, West Virginia again falls to the bottom with its low entrepreneurship and concentrated industry. However, existing businesses are competitive, with few closings and a very high rate of capital investment.

- **Development Capacity:** West Virginia's development resources are poor across the board – with the worst high school and college attainment in the nation. And while energy costs are understandably low, poor bridges and highways are barriers to new industrial development.

For more information on how grades and ranks are calculated, see the Methodology section.
For a detailed explanation of indexes, refer to the individual index section.

WHERE WEST VIRGINIA RANKS – MEASURE BY MEASURE

ECONOMIC PERFORMANCE INDEX MEASURES

		50th	40th	30th	20th	10th	1st
Employment	Long-Term Employment Growth (41)						
	Short-Term Employment Growth (15)						
	Unemployment Rate (50)						
	Unemployment Duration (47)						
Earnings & Job Quality	Average Annual Pay (34)						
	Average Annual Pay Growth (45)						
	Health Coverage (40)						
Equity	Poverty Rate (48)						
	Income Distribution (37)						
	Income Distribution Change (3)						
	Rural/Urban Disparity (16)						
Environmental, Social & Health Conditions	Air Quality (18)						
	Superfund Dumpsites (12)						
	Hazardous Waste Generation (47)						
	Surface Water Discharge (43)						
	Infant Mortality (41)						
	Crime Rate (1)						
	Teen Pregnancy (25)						
	Heart Disease (50)						
	Cancer Cases (49)						
	Infectious Diseases (5)						

BUSINESS VITALITY INDEX MEASURES

		50th	40th	30th	20th	10th	1st
Competitiveness of Existing Business	Traded Sector Strength (26)						
	Change in Traded Sector Strength (28)						
	Business Closings (16)						
	Manufacturing Capital Investment (8)						
Entrepreneurial Energy	New Companies (28)						
	Change in New Companies (43)						
	New Business Job Growth (40)						
Structural Diversity	Sectoral Diversity (42)						
	Dynamic Diversity (35)						

DEVELOPMENT CAPACITY INDEX MEASURES

		50th	40th	30th	20th	10th	1st
Human Resources	High School Graduation (18)						
	High School Education Attainment (50)						
	College Education Attainment (50)						
Technology Resources	Ph.D. Scientists & Engineers in Workforce (44)						
	Science/Engineering Graduate Students (43)						
	Patents Issued (41)						
	University Research & Development (46)						
	Federal Research & Development (29)						
	SBIR Grants (49)						
Financial Resources	Commercial Bank Deposits (18)						
	Loans to Deposits (37)						
	Loans to Equity (41)						
	Commercial & Industrial Loans (39)						
	Comm. & Ind. Loans to Total Loans (45)						
	Venture Capital Investments (37)						
	SBIC Financings (2)						
Infrastructure & Amenity Resources	Highway Deficiency (40)						
	Bridge Deficiency (46)						
	Urban Mass Transit Availability (35)						
	Energy Cost (7)						
	Sewage Treatment Needs (44)						
	Urban Housing Costs (17)						
	Health Professional Shortage Areas (43)						
	Tourism Spending (46)						

TAX & FISCAL SYSTEM INDEX MEASURES

		50th	40th	30th	20th	10th	1st
	Total Tax & Fiscal System Score (24)						
	Fiscal Stability & Balanced Revenue (35)						
	Tax Fairness (38)						
	Fiscal Equalization (7)						

WISCONSIN 1994 REPORT CARD

ECONOMIC PERFORMANCE	A
Employment	A
Earnings & Job Quality	B
Equity	A

BUSINESS VITALITY	D
Business Competitiveness	C
Entrepreneurial Energy	D
Structural Diversity	C

DEVELOPMENT CAPACITY	A
Human Resources	B
Technology Resources	C
Financial Resources	B
Infrastructure & Amenity Resources	B

Tax & Fiscal System	+

- **Economic Performance:** Wisconsin's performance was the third best in the nation. Led by the seventh lowest unemployment rate, strong job growth, and outstanding health benefits. Wisconsin claims both strong job opportunity and job quality. Also, the benefits of the state's economy are spread evenly.

- **Business Vitality:** In contrast to its strong economic performance, Wisconsin's vitality is weak. Businesses score below the median on structural diversity, and with low scores on new firm formation, entrepreneurial energy is weak.

- **Development Capacity:** Wisconsin's development resources are strong across the board, giving the state one of the best overall scores in the nation. Infrastructure resources are particularly strong, marked by top twenty rankings for bridges, mass transit, energy cost, and sewage treatment. With the seventh best high school graduation rate, human resources are also strong.

Five Year Grade Trends

	1990	1991	1992	1993	1994
A					
B					
C					
D					
F					

Key

Economic Performance	——
Business Vitality	————
Development Capacity	- - -

For more information on how grades and ranks are calculated, see the Methodology section.
For a detailed explanation of indexes, refer to the individual index section.

The Corporation for Enterprise Development

WHERE WISCONSIN RANKS – MEASURE BY MEASURE

Scale: 50th 40th 30th 20th 10th 1st

ECONOMIC PERFORMANCE INDEX MEASURES

Employment
- Long-Term Employment Growth (14)
- Short-Term Employment Growth (24)
- Unemployment Rate (7)
- Unemployment Duration (8)

Earnings & Job Quality
- Average Annual Pay (28)
- Average Annual Pay Growth (17)
- Health Coverage (4)

Equity
- Poverty Rate (13)
- Income Distribution (5)
- Income Distribution Change (26)
- Rural/Urban Disparity (22)

Environmental, Social & Health Conditions
- Air Quality (40)
- Superfund Dumpsites (36)
- Hazardous Waste Generation (17)
- Surface Water Discharge (15)
- Infant Mortality (16)
- Crime Rate (13)
- Teen Pregnancy (10)
- Heart Disease (18)
- Cancer Cases (20)
- Infectious Diseases (15)

BUSINESS VITALITY INDEX MEASURES

Competitiveness of Existing Business
- Traded Sector Strength (15)
- Change in Traded Sector Strength (40)
- Business Closings (6)
- Manufacturing Capital Investment (30)

Entrepreneurial Energy
- New Companies (46)
- Change in New Companies (35)
- New Business Job Growth (16)

Structural Diversity
- Sectoral Diversity (24)
- Dynamic Diversity (32)

DEVELOPMENT CAPACITY INDEX MEASURES

Human Resources
- High School Graduation (7)
- High School Education Attainment (19)
- College Education Attainment (25)

Technology Resources
- Ph.D. Scientists & Engineers in Workforce (41)
- Science/Engineering Graduate Students (17)
- Patents Issued (13)
- University Research & Development (10)
- Federal Research & Development (41)
- SBIR Grants (24)

Financial Resources
- Commercial Bank Deposits (25)
- Loans to Deposits (26)
- Loans to Equity (18)
- Commercial & Industrial Loans (19)
- Comm. & Ind. Loans to Total Loans (13)
- Venture Capital Investments (33)
- SBIC Financings (7)

Infrastructure & Amenity Resources
- Highway Deficiency (21)
- Bridge Deficiency (20)
- Urban Mass Transit Availability (15)
- Energy Cost (11)
- Sewage Treatment Needs (14)
- Urban Housing Costs (20)
- Health Professional Shortage Areas (29)
- Tourism Spending (43)

TAX & FISCAL SYSTEM INDEX MEASURES

- Total Tax & Fiscal System Score (11)
- Fiscal Stability & Balanced Revenue (11)
- Tax Fairness (17)
- Fiscal Equalization (21)

Scale: 50th 40th 30th 20th 10th 1st

WYOMING 1994 REPORT CARD

ECONOMIC PERFORMANCE — C

Employment C
Earnings & Job Quality .... D
Equity .... A

BUSINESS VITALITY — C

Business Competitiveness .... B
Entrepreneurial Energy .... D
Structural Diversity C

DEVELOPMENT CAPACITY — D

Human Resources .... B
Technology Resources C
Financial Resources .... D
Infrastructure & Amenity Resources C

Tax & Fiscal System — –

- **Economic Performance:** Wyoming's performance is mixed. Unemployment is low, but long-term job growth is the nation's worst. Also, health coverage is good, but average pay is low and growing slowly. On the positive side, Wyoming ranks fourth in the U.S. on measures of equity and second on environmental quality.

- **Business Vitality:** With a sharp downturn in entrepreneurial energy, marked by a steep drop in the growth of new firm formations, Wyoming fell a grade from last year. Competitiveness of existing businesses remains strong.

- **Development Capacity:** After average but steady grades over the last five years, Wyoming's grade dropped this year. While technology and financial resources remain poor, infrastructure falls to a C. Human resources remain the one strong point, but with a drop in college attainment, it is no longer outstanding.

Five Year Grade Trends

	1990	1991	1992	1993	1994

Key
Economic Performance ———
Business Vitality ▒▒▒
Development Capacity – – –

For more information on how grades and ranks are calculated, see the Methodology section.
For a detailed explanation of indexes, refer to the individual index section.

WHERE WYOMING RANKS – MEASURE BY MEASURE

Scale: 50th — 40th — 30th — 20th — 10th — 1st

ECONOMIC PERFORMANCE INDEX MEASURES

Employment
- Long-Term Employment Growth (50)
- Short-Term Employment Growth (39)
- Unemployment Rate (15)
- Unemployment Duration (3)

Earnings & Job Quality
- Average Annual Pay (41)
- Average Annual Pay Growth (50)
- Health Coverage (17)

Equity
- Poverty Rate (9)
- Income Distribution (8)
- Income Distribution Change (28)
- Rural/Urban Disparity (14)

Environmental, Social & Health Conditions
- Air Quality (1)
- Superfund Dumpsites (32)
- Hazardous Waste Generation (3)
- Surface Water Discharge (11)
- Infant Mortality (46)
- Crime Rate (15)
- Teen Pregnancy (19)
- Heart Disease (10)
- Cancer Cases (9)
- Infectious Diseases (21)

BUSINESS VITALITY INDEX MEASURES

Competitiveness of Existing Business
- Traded Sector Strength (29)
- Change in Traded Sector Strength (4)
- Business Closings (40)
- Manufacturing Capital Investment (9)

Entrepreneurial Energy
- New Companies (5)
- Change in New Companies (44)
- New Business Job Growth (47)

Structural Diversity
- Sectoral Diversity (39)
- Dynamic Diversity (23)

DEVELOPMENT CAPACITY INDEX MEASURES

Human Resources
- High School Graduation (9)
- High School Education Attainment (10)
- College Education Attainment (32)

Technology Resources
- Ph.D. Scientists & Engineers in Workforce (18)
- Science/Engineering Graduate Students (11)
- Patents Issued (47)
- University Research & Development (28)
- Federal Research & Development (39)
- SBIR Grants (48)

Financial Resources
- Commercial Bank Deposits (15)
- Loans to Deposits (46)
- Loans to Equity (44)
- Commercial & Industrial Loans (38)
- Comm. & Ind. Loans to Total Loans (27)
- Venture Capital Investments (37)
- SBIC Financings (44)

Infrastructure & Amenity Resources
- Highway Deficiency (7)
- Bridge Deficiency (6)
- Urban Mass Transit Availability (50)
- Energy Cost (5)
- Sewage Treatment Needs (50)
- Urban Housing Costs (45)
- Health Professional Shortage Areas (45)
- Tourism Spending (4)

TAX & FISCAL SYSTEM INDEX MEASURES

- Total Tax & Fiscal System Score (44)
- Fiscal Stability & Balanced Revenue (48)
- Tax Fairness (43)
- Fiscal Equalization (3)

Scale: 50th — 40th — 30th — 20th — 10th — 1st